BRITISH RAILWAYS

PAST and PRESENT

No 11

BRITISH RAILWAYS PAST & PRESENT No 11: NORTH YORKSHIRE (PART 1) – This book presents a detailed examination of the changing face of the railways in the region depicted in this map, which includes locations featured in the photographs or mentioned in the text. The pictures have been chosen to provide a balanced view, including railways which are still in use or being developed, together with scenes where the lines have been closed and either abandoned or redeveloped since the 'past' pictures were taken.

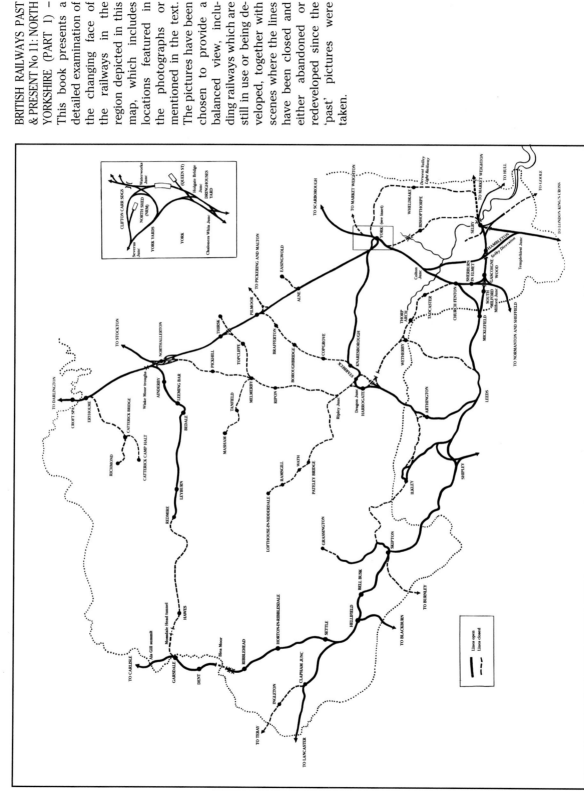

BRITISH RAILWAYS

PAST and PRESENT

No 11

North Yorkshire (Part 1)
York and Selby, the Dales, and Skipton to Garsdale

Alan R. Thompson & Ken Groundwater

Silver Link Publishing Ltd

First published in December 1991

British Library Cataloguing in Publication Data
British railways past and present
No. 11: North Yorkshire
Pt. 1: York and Selby, the Dales and Skipton to
Garsdale
I. Thompson, Alan R. II. Groundwater, Ken
385.0941

ISBN 0 947971 71 8

Silver Link Publishing Ltd
The Trundle
Ringstead Road
Great Addington
Kettering
Northants NN14 4BW

Maps drawn by Christina Siviter

Typeset by The TypeFoundry, Northampton.
Printed and bound in Great Britain by
Woolnough Bookbinding Ltd, Irthlingborough,
Northants

NOTE: Photographs credited *JWA* were taken by
J.W. Armstrong, *ART* by Alan R. Thompson and *KG* by
Ken Groundwater, while those credited *BR* appear by
courtesy of British Railways. All other credits are
given in full.

**FIRST ELECTRIC TRAIN IN PUBLIC SERVICE NORTH OF YORK: It was intended to catch this historic scene in the
vicinity of York (or at least on the ECML within the boundaries of this book!), but in the event power supply
problems in the Newcastle area delayed the proving trials and the first train – planned for the morning of 10 June
1991 – ran unannounced in the afternoon. The train in question was the 15.30 (1NO5) King's Cross-Newcastle
service, and is seen here considerably north of York, at Lamesley, Gateshead. Most people had given up hope of
an electric service on the 10th and the running of 1NO5 was an almost spontaneous event, catching out most of the
photographic fraternity. Here, then, is history being made after five years of planning.** *KG*

CONTENTS

BIBLIOGRAPHY

Railways Around Harrogate *by Martin Bairstow & David Beeken (M. Bairstow)*

Railway Stations of the North-East *by K. Hoole (David & Charles)*

Railways Memories of York *by Ernest Sanderson (Bellcode)*

BR Steam Motive Power Depots (NER) *by Paul Bolger (Ian Allan)*

What Happened to Steam (various additions) *by P.B. Hands (P.B. Hands)*

Locomotives of the LNER (various parts) *(RCTS)*

The Wensleydale Branch *by C.T. Goode (Oakwood Press)*

The Skipton & Ilkley Line *by F.W. Smith & Donald Binns (Wyvern Publications)*

The Railway and its Passengers *by D.N. Smith (David & Charles)*

North Of Leeds *by Peter E. Baughan (Roundhouse Books)*

North Eastern Record *by John Proud and other NERA authors (HMRS)*

INTRODUCTION

The anchor-pin of this staggeringly beautiful area of England is York, with all its trappings of grandeur and history aptly linking past civilisations with the present. It was the natural Northern Capital, and its fading from importance has been seen by many as the start of the present-day commercial imbalance between North and South, a situation only now redressing itself with the North clearly that one step ahead environmentally. But discounting the mysteries of commerce and politics, it is pleasing that one commodity has remained firmly embedded in the North, one that I suspect London once thought it would (and still ultimately may) acquire — management of the North Eastern railways. Even as recently as the '70s we have seen 'attempts' upon York (remember BR's stillborn 'Field' Organisation proposals?).

Just as York is surrounded by battlefields — a sure indicator of its important strategic position — so the early railway builders found it a convenient crossroads where the Wharfe and the Derwent arrived in the Vale of York. Criss-crossed by a good many of the world's first commercially viable railways, Yorkshire quickly became an early stronghold of locomotive and carriage construction, a development due in no small measure to the proximity of Durham and Northumberland and their railway entrepreneurs.

Yet beyond the pockets of heavy engineering and across the Vale to the west lies the quiet beauty of the Dales, and in particular the Craven and Ribblesdale regions. The arrival of the train amongst these rough northern diamonds opened up the area to both factory worker and nobility alike, and few Victorians could disguise their excitement when making a quick escape from St Pancras via a luxurious and lumbering Midland Pullman.

It was, however, a sad and a sobering business to revisit today such places as Hellifield, and compare a Mike Mensing print of a far-off busy August Bank Holiday in 1959. When you see the picture it is clear that there was a Dales station still reflecting the constant activity of both its steam trains and its local people, and it is almost — but not quite — possible to smell an oily whiff from a Fowler 'Crab' or hear the distinctive buzz of a Belpaire.

The changes portrayed at Hellifield on the one hand, and on the other at little Bell Busk (on what might be described the 'junior slopes' of the 'Long Drag') all serve to contrast sharply with a towering Billiard Hall overlooking the grimy Ouse and catering for the demands of the more industrial workforce of a smoky Selby at the century's turn. Crossing Selby's vast coalfield we find wide tracts of railway

HOLGATE JUNCTION, YORK: All signalling enthusiasts will associate the pre-1951 scene at this location with this fine display of NER slotted signals. To others it was simply an excellent place to spend a sunny day watching trains of every hue, with unexpected foreign engines bound to appear eventually! A not uncommon pairing at this point is illustrated here by John Armstrong, who devoted many hours of photography to this junction over a 30-year span (see also pages 108-9). It is 1949 and 'A4' 'Pacific' No 60008 has recently been renumbered from '8' and renamed *Dwight D. Eisenhower* (ex-*Golden Shuttle*). Still 'garter blue', she appears to have been delayed by a conflicting movement ahead and is met by an LMS Class '4F' 0-6-0 No 43906, displaying tablet No 291 and hauling an additional train back to the Midlands. Holgate platform was still in regular use at this time for racecourse excursion trains and Holgate Junction groundframe cabin, seen between the engines, was electronically interlocked with the large Locomotive Yard cabin (as shown on page 102). *JWA*

Another 42 years of endless railway traffic at this point has brought Holgate into the age of computer-controlled signalling, overhead electrification and a much simplified track layout. Even Holgate Bridge, carrying the main Harrogate road, has been altered, jacked up 1 foot to cater for the overhead line equipment now in situ. On 7 April 1991 a King's Cross–York service is being propelled back into the downside holding sidings, near Dringhouses, there to await its return service. When this book is published the advent of Class '91' electrics and Mark IV coaching stock should be a familiar sight along the entire ECML. Their takeover will introduce a quieter era, the whistle of the HST power cars becoming a less familiar sound just as the 'Deltic' roar is now also an ECML memory. The church alone remains in mute testimony to their passing. *ART*

acreage engulfing former arable plains around Milford and Monk Fryston, where the LNER once handed over its precious minerals and metals to the LMS for onward transit to the steelmasters of Sheffield. At these locations, once the heartland of 'railway mania', we were astonished by the way that nature had quietly reclaimed so much that was ploughed up in long thin strips 150 years ago in a maelstrom of speculative fury.

North Yorkshire, like many less densely populated areas, tells the all-too-familiar tale of cuts and economies associated with the work of the man ironically labelled the 'great and good Doctor'. But Yorkshire, like its people, will not easily lie down, and today there are everywhere the undercurrents of rail renaissance. There is much to encourage those who care for this green county and have long been sickened by the poison and slaughter of our peripheral public highways! Of the more advanced schemes we can look forward to passengers again traversing Wensleydale to alight at Aysgarth for the 'falls', and eventually to travel on to Hawes Junction (with apologies to Garsdale).

Further south, Ripon's rail revival has much strong support, also now fired by the change in the 'official' Government stance towards railways. Let's hope that one day we shall once again see this northern city back where it belongs, on the railway map!

Whatever reopenings may occur, we will all now look back upon the battle to save the Settle & Carlisle as the watershed of the railways' years of decline. That fight, which brought all caring people together, surprised both Government Ministers and BR senior management and gave democracy a great boost. So look closely at the 'present' scenes at Ribblehead, Bell Busk or Sherwood Brow and reflect on what might have been, and how different it would all look without the shining strips of steel leading towards the hills, or without the MR mileposts, still today optimistically telling us the distance from London St Pancras!

The high proportion of 'past' illustrations attributed to the late John W. Armstrong needs some explanation. The authors were part of a syndicate invited to assess the JWA collection in 1988 by the then custodian, who wished to see that John's last request, that his collection be kept intact, was upheld. John dreaded the fate that befell his friend's collection (E.E. Smith), and knew that his life's work could similarly be 'spread to the four winds' in the wrong hands. Thus what became the J.W. Armstrong Trust acquired the collection to maintain it for future generations of historians. The authors would therefore like to thank the other members of the Trust for not only subscribing to this appropriate application of John's work, but for also giving encouragement and assistance in the preparation and checking of the caption data.

John Midcalf gave freely of his vast knowledge of signalling matters and ably acted as guide and chauffeur on not a few jaunts into 'deepest' Yorkshire. Dave Tyreman contributed in typical selfless style by not only checking captions but also searching out photographs of rarer locations from his own collection. For locations demanding lengthy research around the Selby area we would like to thank Roger Hill. Robert Anderson of York's Central Photographic Unit was very patient with badly defined requests, but always found the subject and, together with Stuart Rankin, turned up many fine prints. John Edgington, once of the NRM staff, cooperated with our requests and himself produced some excellent 'past' Harrogate views. John Spencer Gilks gave a day from his busy schedule to allow a search to be made of the extensive collection belonging to Ryedale Audio-Visual at Nawton, Finally, Chris Dickinson and Bob Bone, the last BR Area Managers for the Newcastle and York areas respectively, helped considerably by granting facilities and providing topical information concerning their areas of responsibility; we wish them well in their new roles following BR's 'Reorganisation for Quality'.

It only remains for us to pay tribute to certain young ladies who made the preparation of the manuscript that much more enjoyable, and who so ably translated spidery and unintelligible notes: Allison Docherty, Eileen Allen, Dorothy Robinson and Louise Groundwater (with her mother Pauline frequently acting as interpreter!). A word of thanks also to June Thompson for allowing her holiday journeys south to be used to circumnavigate most of the county of Yorkshire!

Ken Groundwater
Gateshead

Alan R. Thompson
Penshaw, Co Durham

Skipton to Grassington and Garsdale

SKIPTON MR had to wait until 30 July 1849 before a start was made to push the line up towards Ribblesdale and, as a joint venture by the Midland and 'Little North Western' railways, it went only as far north as a junction with the Lancaster & Carlisle at Ingleton. It wasn't, however, an equal partnership, and the Midland Railway looked for its own route culminating in the Settle & Carlisle. Here is the station in May 1967; two crews exchange greetings while the large 'Potts of Leeds' platform clock eyes the proceedings as the hours tick away for BR steam traction.

Twenty-three years later, in May 1990, the wooden constructions for the various station shops have been removed, showing the fine local stonework to better advantage. The station demands something more spectacular than a Class '142' DMU, and the surroundings unfortunately tend to emphasise the great void between the past great Steam Age and a West Yorkshire 'Pacer' set. *Both KG*

SKIPTON NER: The NER had running rights into Skipton via the joint MR/NER station at Ilkley, and entered the town over Carleton Road Bridge before dropping down a twisting 1 in 85 gradient to come to rest in the NER platforms shown here in the mid-'fifties, when 'J39' and 'B16' Class engines predominated on this route. Here we see a Class 'J39' with a return Blackpool–Harrogate–York excursion about to leave platform 5 and attack Carleton Road Bank. Different classes were tried on this difficult gradient – 'B1s', 'K1s', 'K3s' – but the authorities always returned to the 'J39s' and 'B16s', Skipton receiving an allocation when it came under the auspices of the BR (NE) Area. *JWA*

Today, Skipton continues to be under the control of the Leeds-based Regional Railway Sector, but platform 5 is derelict and used only by the aggregates sub-sector of Railfreight for access to the ex-MR main line with traffic from the quarry at Swinden along the Grassington branch. *KG*

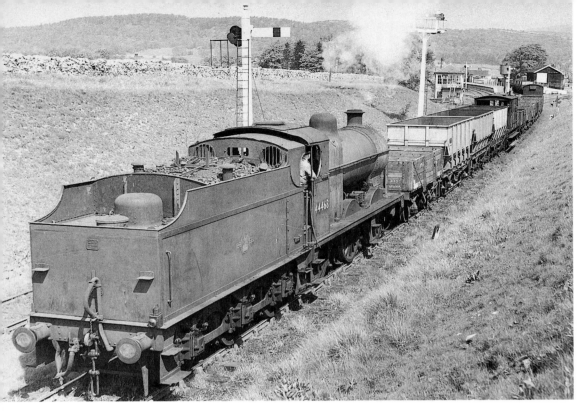

GRASSINGTON: Many of us who chased the last sunbeams of steam on the LM Region would inevitably have made our way to the Grassington branch to see BR Standard Class '4' engines performing the last rites, until which time this byway had been mostly ignored. One person who didn't leave it too late was John Spencer Gilks, a photographer perhaps more associated with recording London area scenes in the 1950s; on 25 May 1960 John caught a Fowler tender-cab-fitted Class '4F' No 44468 at Grassington shunting a mixed rake consisting mainly of 'highfits' and 21-ton hoppers.

He returned to the same scene on 26 January 1989, finding the location with difficulty; the cutting now accommodates some makeshift sheep pens and hay bales, while a housing estate has advanced from the station area and looks likely to advance further. The line of trees and a large rooftop funnel remain as common features. *Both John Spencer Gilks/Ryedale AV*

BELL BUSK station, closed on 4 May 1959, was once the alighting point for tourists who were met by pony and trap and taken the half a dozen miles to Malhamdale for the customary circuit of Craven and all its natural beauty. At about the time of its closure it was brought to the attention of the railway press via some powerful imagery from the camera of the late Eric Treacy. Our group of past pictures catches a scenario that underlined the then strong dominance in the community of railway station officials and local government officers. In this instance Mr G. B. Drayson, MP for Skipton and District, is visiting Bell Busk to be seen 'out and caring' by the Skipton press, and is taken on a tour of the tiny station conducted by acting Station Master Willie Bateson. (With his back to the camera is Mr C. Beasley, the Tory agent for the area.) *Courtesy of Mr & Mrs Pye of Skipton.*

Since its demise as an operating station, Bell Busk continued to hit the headlines, and in 1984 won an AA award as 'a unique building in the North' due in no small way to the efforts of Mr Kenneth Bristow, its owner and renovator between 1978 and 1988, who converted the property into a fine lineside guest house. The new owners, Mr and Mrs Philpot, stand alongside guest Peter McCallum on 11 May 1990, and it is plainly evident that the location is a must for anyone with a bad case of Settle-&-Carlisle-itis! The dining room now occupies part of the platform, the lounge was once the booking office and the former covered area of platform has been adapted as a games room. 'Little North Western' Railway relics abound and with the current presence of 'Cumbrian Mountain Expresses' the scene is complete as an extremely civilised setting. *KG*

Willie Bateson and Mr Drayson inspect the MR–style gas lamps. The sack barrow behind displays the legend 'Bell Busk: Tare 1-2'. Also seen are the station steps for assisting the infirm down on to the low platforms, and the customary publicity for 'The English Lakes', 'The Pass of Glencoe' and Left Luggage conditions. *Courtesy of Mr & Mrs Pye of Skipton*

Mr Drayson chats to the signalman about life in a Midland Railway signal box. One wonders where the box nameboard went! *Courtesy of Mr & Mrs Pye of Skipton*

At a time when **Hellifield** is being encouraged to blossom as the 'Gateway to the Settle & Carlisle', with its tourist facilities and a field research centre, it is perhaps timely to look briefly at its recent past when there were still bookstalls and 1st and 3rd class waiting rooms.

Up and running as a station by 1880, it was designed to reflect its importance as a major Midland Railway junction with the expectation of Royalty calling to visit the nobility at nearby Brocklesby Hall. Up until the Second World War more than half of the town's workforce were employed by 'the railway' and a not inconsiderable number were involved in catering for hungry passengers prior to train dining cars. A cold luncheon basket could be purchased here for 3 shillings, and besides a half chicken would include a half bottle of burgundy!

Caught up in the middle of the competition between the Midland and the LNWR, Hellifield was the location for detaching and attaching through coaches for such places as Liverpool, Manchester, and Blackburn. When in 1880 the cost of supplying all of Hellifield's facilities was totted up it came to over £20,000. Trains eventually originated at Hellifield for Hawes, Bradford, Leeds, Lancaster and Carlisle, and between 1901 and 1914 the station was handling 90 passenger trains daily and 200,000 wagon exchanges yearly.

The engine shed had an allocation of 28 locomotives and two vital snow ploughs. With the grouping into four main-line companies of all the railways in Britain in 1923, the Midland route became 'second-fiddle' to the West Coast (LNWR) route, and the decline of Hellifield's importance began. Here are some more recent dates of interest:

10 Sept 1962 Blackburn–Hellifield passenger service ceased
17 June 1963 Hellifield Motive Power Depot closed
29 April 1964 Hellifield closed to goods traffic
4 May 1970 Stopping passenger services along the Settle & Carlisle withdrawn leaving only these stations open: Long Preston, Settle, Appleby and Hellifield.

During the late 1970s we have seen an incredible reversal begin, spearheaded by the Dalesrail excursions culminating in the 1989 decision to retain the route.

The following 1990 views belie the possibilities at Hellifield, as it can be seen that neglect and an expected total shut-down have left the long cloister-like arrangement of arched cast-iron supports with their columns encrusted with a century of soot and weathering, the station unstaffed and boarded up, and the chilly Pennine wind whistling along the platforms to conjure up thoughts of some railway drama associated with the wild weather in these parts.

HELLIFIELD (1): Derby-built 'Compound' No 41068 (of Leeds Holbeck shed) pauses at Hellifield south end in about 1950 having manfully brought in a Carlisle–Leeds stopping service from over the 'Long Drag'. Stanier Class '8F' No 48505 awaits the 'board' for the exit from Hellifield MPD roads. *JWA*

The roof of the coaling stage having now gone from the Hellifield horizon (along with all the other equipment needed for a fully commissioned loco shed), the magnificent Midland wrought-iron tapestries remain as a reminder of the former glory of this once busy junction station. On 18 May 1991 a Leeds-bound Class '144' DMU pulls away from a dilapidated platform. *ART*

HELLIFIELD (2): It's 3 August 1959, at 11.45 am, and the guard has another 10 minutes to load into his van the contents of the trolley before Stanier '4' 2-6-4T No 42542 will be 'right away' with the 11.55 am 'slow' to Carlisle. Photographer Michael Mensing says by way of recollection that 'I spent the entire Bank Holiday dodging showers and supposing that at any minute the sun would surely shine . . . but in true Settle–Carlisle manner – it didn't'. Nevertheless, the weather fails to detract from this vintage scene. *Michael Mensing*

In May 1990 we see the bay in even duller conditions. Its day done, it is bypassed by a Class '31' diesel at the head of the 09.41 service from Carlisle to Leeds. *KG*

16

HELLIFIELD (3): Shortage of motive power on the same day, 3 August 1959, sees ex-MR Class '4F' No 43960 pressed into service over the 'Long Drag' with an excursion from the Blackburn direction. *Michael Mensing*

In May 1991 a Leeds–Morecambe Class '142' railcar departs as Hellifield prepares for its predicted renaissance as a Settle & Carlisle study centre. *ART*

SHERWOOD BROW (I): Crossing the skew bridge on 3 August 1959, the 15.40 Bradford Forster Square–Carlisle is led by 'Crab' 2-6-0 No 42770, being elevated to 'higher grade' duty for the Bank Holiday weekend. *Michael Mensing*
Just before a lot of detail became totally leaf-obscured, on 18 May 1991, 'Super Sprinter' No 156472 arrives at the same location with a midday Leeds–Carlisle new-look service. This is now the only way to record this extraordinary route – no longer can enthusiasts look out from windows/door toplights and photograph as they go. *ART*

18

SHERWOOD BROW (2): Having just crossed the bridge at Sherwood Brow on the same day, the 16.4 Garsdale–Hellifield 'stopper' approaches a location 238½ miles from St Pancras and the crew of Stanier '4' 2-6-4 No 42491 will be grateful that they are not required to go the full distance! *Michael Mensing*

On 11 May 1990 a wider angle view witnesses the 12.42 Carlisle–Leeds train passing an almost afforested u side, whilst on the opposite side the removal of telegraph poles has completely changed the character of the scen and resulted in the new popularity of the area beyond being dubbed the 'Shap Mound' of the Settle route . . . *KG*

HORTON IN RIBBLESDALE: Because this location has received so much exposure in the railway press over the years we asked Mike Mensing for something different and, as usual, he came up with the goods! Here at Horton-in-Ribblesdale in the northern corner of the up side platform is a fine vignette of small details that show beyond doubt the extent of 'tender loving care' lavished upon the station by the staff (and incidentally proving that Settle station was no exception!). The station nameboard and heraldry are perhaps not official handiwork, but most readers will agree that they fitted well into the neat garden plot. The topmost display publicises the town's four major legacies, ie transport, lime burning, sheep and dairy farming, and finally the ancient church of c1160. *Michael Mensing*

On 12 May 1990 we found the outbuilding gone, but an attempt to restore the small garden by the 'Friends of the S&C' is most pleasing. *KG*

RIBBLEHEAD: Call it what you like – Batty Moss, Batty Wife or even Ribblehead Viaduct – almost everyone north of Watford (and quite a lot south) will have read about the emotive struggle centred around this Grade II listed monument that is now officially listed as one of the six wonders of the north. Leading across the flat bed of the upper Ribble towards '. . . that terrible place called Blea Moor . . .' it stands between the three peaks of Whernside, Ingleborough and Penyghent, acting as a superb focal point of all three. It is always an awesome place to walk under with its strange habit of challenging the Pennine winds to blow a bit unnaturally around its support legs. A quarter of a mile long on a gentle curve, it has 24 arches, reaches 105 feet above the usually boggy moorland below, and must be experienced from below to be placed properly in perspective.

Tales abound, and author Bill Mitchell of Settle has collected most of them and has even written a book concerning simply 'the Viaduct'! The most famous involves old George Routh, the ganger of the section in 1956-1960, who was heard relating the day that the wind blew the cap from his head, off the viaduct, under an arch, and back on to his head. George complained it landed 'wrang way round'!

Looking towards Whernside's mass, 'Jubilee' 4-6-0 No 45593 *Kolhapur* battles against a strong headwind in August 1966 with the Nottingham–Glasgow service. In May 1991, in similar dull and threatening weather conditions, a Class '156' crosses the viaduct travelling in the opposite direction over this now singled stretch with a Carlisle–Leeds service. *Both ART*

SALT LAKE CITY COTTAGES: It is said that the cottages giving their name to this overbridge (about 1 mile south of Ribblehead) have a lineage going back to the Midland Managers outbased in this area to oversee the construction progress/delays at that 'terrible place' beyond, Blea Moor! Even as recently as 1980 George Horner (senior), one of the line's characters and a signalman at Blea Moor, lived here and thus the railway connections continued into the 1980s. On 3 August 1959 ' Britannia' 'Pacific' No 70044 *Earl Haig* is train engine on the down 'Waverley' express being assisted by Stanier 'Black 5' No 44675 with the mass of Penyghent strung out along the skyline. *Michael Mensing*

The same scene on 13 May 1990 sees two Class '31' engines re-enacting the action with the 13.45 Leeds–Carlisle service. *Peter McCallum*

DENT: In 1964 it was still possible to get lonely Dent station to yourself — for an entire day! Kingmoor 'Black Five' No 44689 has turned up in business-like manner at the head of the 08.00 Hunslet–Carlisle Class '8' goods; the crew, having negotiated the majority of the 'Long Drag', know they only have Risehill to endure before 44689 will burst out upon the broad sweep of Garsdale and 'dunk' the scoop for a long drink on the 'level'. Through the swirling smokescreen can be seen the signal cabin that stood here for so long to guard this long section, with Denthead Viaduct behind in

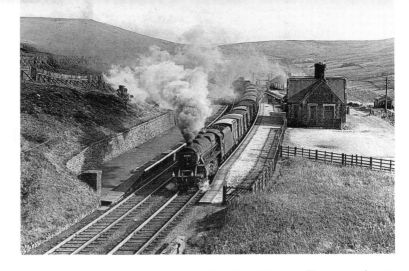

the far distance. The snow fences appear to have been fairly well maintained up to this time by comparison to their current remains. *ART*

On 3 March 1990 Class '58' No 58036 was a celebrity guest, borrowed from the Railfreight Coal sub-sector during a spell of 'promotional' foreign-power guesting in 1990. Here it is about to pass below the 'Coal Road' bridge at Dent, whilst assisting Class '47' No 47453 at the head of the 08.25 Leeds–Carlisle train. *Peter J. Robinson*

Dent was picked out for much attention for evangelists in the 'sixties – here is an example from 1967. It was in many ways a strange and inappropriate location for this sort of treatment, for few other places could be considered intrinsically more spiritual. Yet today, how appropriate – since the S&C indeed 'rose again', hopefully 'for evermore'. *KG*

GARSDALE TROUGHS (1): Celebrated as the highest main-line troughs in the world, at 1,145 feet above sea level, they were situated on one of the few level sections in this remote and spectacular region between Hawes Junction and Risehill Tunnel. The frequency of trains at one time was such that those at the rear of a procession caught the troughs still slowly filling from the hillside tank, and a further water stop at either Blea Moor, on the up, or Kirkby Stephen, on the down, would be needed to replenish the thirsting and hard-worked engine. In our 1950 view we can see that LMS 'Crab' No 42819 has the benefit of a full trough and the fireman is no doubt heavily engaged in judging the moment to wind up the scoop. The large permanent way cabin associated with maintenance of this section is at the left, and the filler tank opposite took its water from a nearby beck coming down off Widdale Fell on the right. *JWA*

Our visit on 15 May 1990 was at a time when proper trains (ie with engines at the front) were still employed on the Carlisle–Leeds service! Here No 31416 passes over the site of the troughs with the 09.35 from Carlisle in typical Pennine rain. One remaining tell-tale sign, down at rail level, is the large paving flag drainage covers in the cess, still canted in towards the line in a way that would have encouraged water overflow to drain away. *KG*

GARSDALE TROUGHS (2): It was supposedly unusual for LNWR Class 'G' ('Super D') 0-8-0 goods engines to get as far as Skipton, but for one to travel the length of the line to Carlisle was extremely rare. In about 1949 John Armstrong caught this scene near the north end of Garsdale troughs. *JWA*

The same location on 15 May 1990 was photographed in much less misty conditions. The lower-quadrant distant on the down line is now an upper quadrant, but the fog cabin is still just evident behind No 31449 at the head of the 08.27 Leeds–Carlisle service. *KG*

GARSDALE STATION (I): From the slopes of Mossdale Moor a moment in 1950 is frozen by John Armstrong. Class 'G5' 0-4-4T No 67312 has brought in the 07.15 service from Northallerton and, without turning, awaits the return journey at 10.50, whilst a Fowler 'Crab' 2-6-0 No 42834 of Kingmoor MPD hurries by with a surprisingly well-stocked tender on the last phase of the gruelling climb to Ais Gill. A detailed examination of the scene shows much fascinating detail, not least the style of the signal box name – Garsdale Junction – being still a junction with the ex-NER branch. *JWA*

From 16 March 1959 the NER platform face was no longer needed when the remaining Garsdale–Hawes passenger service ceased. In June 1989 Garsdale signal box is left intact as an emergency block post, the island platform buildings have all but vanished, and Class '47' No 47623 *Vulcan* arrives with the 16.15 Carlisle–Leeds stopping train. *ART*

GARSDALE STATION (2): Ex-MR Class '4F' No 43922 has 'done its stuff' on the climb to Ais Gill in May 1957, and the crew enjoy the luxury of a gaze at the view along Garsdale on the level section approach to the troughs. The Garsdale station porter absent-mindedly attends to the border plants, having seen perhaps thousands of coke wagons trundle past over the years. *John Spencer Gilks/Ryedale AV*

In May 1990 the station is enjoying revitalisation with a minibus connection to Hawes and Sedbergh, and this fact, together with the ram's-head sign of the Yorkshire Dales Park, is well documented on the current station nameboard. The neat flower border, however, has gone, rather negating the caring hours of the porter. *KG*

GARSDALE NER: A bi-directional starting signal allows the 16.10 Northallerton to Garsdale stopping train to drift into Garsdale station on an idyllic summer evening in 1951. The Class 'D20' (ex-NER Class 'R') No 62347 of Northallerton MPD will have exactly 44 minutes to both reverse and prepare for the 94-minute return journey home. The sylvan setting and a golden moment is perhaps enough to excuse several gentlemen's shadows! *JWA*

In June 1989 it can be seen that the Midland siding's exit signal has been shortened and the points – lying in exactly the same way – look unused and, if unsponsored, may well be awaiting lifting. *ART*

GARSDALE TURNTABLE: The stockaded turntable at Garsdale is now part of Settle & Carlisle mythology and very few have not heard the excellent tale about an engine being turned in a strong wind, eventually becoming out of control to such a degree that sand shovelled into the pit was the only way to slow down the now rapidly spinning locomotive. The result was a wind-break stockade, and here we see it in action, with its regular user from the Northallerton branch, Class 'D20' No 62347, being turned prior to return. *JWA*

Only the brick surround marks the spot today, and the removal of the stockade gives a clear view over Dandry Mire 'floated' viaduct. The famous turntable is today re-sited on the Keighley & Worth Valley Railway. *ART*

Wensleydale

LEEMING BAR: Almost 6 miles west of Northallerton lies Leeming Bar on the first section of the line to Hawes opened in March 1848. Unlike the route beyond to the west, the Ainderby–Leeming Bar section had celebrated its centenary before passenger trains ceased operating west to Hawes in April 1954. A year before this date, the mid-morning Sunday service from Northallerton consists more of milk tanks for the dairy farmers along the way than for passengers, who would nevertheless have found the one push-pull converted coach spacious. The station building seen here on the westbound platform was far more substantial that would have seemed necessary, even possessing a large portico supported by pillars. *JWA*

Until 1985 the Leeming Bar–Bedale section remained double-tracked, and our 18 June 1989 view shows the now singled section with Class '37s' *Wensleydale* and *Leyburn* having passed the crossing – then under manual operation — and making for Redmire Quarry with the limestone empties. The station house looks rather the worse for wear. *ART*

LEYBURN (1): Passenger operations to Leyburn began on 18 May 1856, and it was anticipated as the western terminus by the Bedale & Leyburn Railway Company when its Act was passed in August 1853. In 1855 the B&L was swallowed up by big brother NER and Leyburn remained the western terminus. However, in 1865 and again in 1869 the MR, L&Y and LNWR all cast envious eyes at a line within striking distance of their territories. The Midland eventually came closest with its ambitious route over the backbone of the Pennines. But even though the Settle & Carlisle was designed as close as possible to Upper Wensleydale, the connection into Hawes Junction (Garsdale) only came after another 20 years' delay. The MR was then permitted to run through to Leyburn, whilst the NER had running rights to Settle.

Our older view could be said to depict a classic country railway scene: the horse-box in the bay, where at one time six highly acclaimed trainers would make use of NER facilities, and the unhurried porter trundling a sack barrow along to an equally unhurried two-coach set forming a Northallerton service. Not only was this unhurried atmosphere the underlying charm of such stations, it was also the reason it couldn't go on for ever. Today, however, as a freight-only branch, the route to Redmire has accomplished a remarkable 'Houdini' escape act. Having now survived so close to the 21st century, it would be a disaster if our new environmentally conscious world were to let it die. *JWA*

Whilst Redmire limestone passes in the right quantity the branch seems safe, and on 18 June 1989 two Class '37s' are seen passing the station site with empties for the quarry, large trees preventing an exact repeat! The downside platform with its recess into the horse-box bay remains little altered, but not surprisingly the awning has gone with the entire upside platform. *ART*

LEYBURN (2): A view of Leyburn at the east end where once stood the locomotive shed, three water columns and a turntable. In the early 'fifties, with the station nameboard sandwiched between a resident Class 'G5' (over the inspection pit) and a locomotive coal wagon, there is little to suggest that the line might one day survive for a passenger renaissance . . . *JWA*

On 30 June 1989 it can be seen that the loco inspection pit has ironically been retained to do the same job with motor cars — only a distant house roof preserves the continuity between the two scenes. *ART*

HAWES: As already noted, the Wensleydale branch was built in stages with the Leyburn–Hawes section coming late in railway terms, in 1878. The entire branch was single line except for the section between Leeming Bar and Bedale and through certain stations, including Hawes, seen here in April 1950. Having arrived from the east, this is as far as the NER Class 'D20' will go, and, whilst awaiting the balancing working in from Hellifield, the Northallerton driver takes some moments to examine the inside motion of his steed. At this time Northallerton had three other Class 'D20' engines and apart from No 62347 (see also pages 31-2) they were Nos 62359, 62388 and 62391, all regularly seen along Wensleydale. Hawes station was jointly owned by the NER and MR, although designed by Midland architects in their style. A lovely story goes that station staff were originally issued with the uniforms of both companies. One can only imagine the Whitehall farce situation when trains ran at unexpected times . . . ! In the days of mass rail travel a big attraction at Hawes was the Hardraw Scar brass band contest. In 1903, for example, nine excursions brought over 3,000 visitors here from as far as Manchester and Newcastle. *JWA*

We found that on 1 June 1989 it was impossible to reconstruct the exact view, but what was pleasing was the buzz of activity around the station, now a tourist information centre, and at the goods shed, an Upper Dales Folk Museum — and very much worth a visit! The third photograph (1950, *JWA*) shows a 'joint' gas lamp and the rear of the main station building, goods shed, and a very busy goods yard. *ART*

But the railway at Hawes, and Wensleydale in general will not lie down, and the Wensleydale Railway Association formed in 1990 had raised over £1,000 in only six weeks to carry out a preliminary survey with the notion of re-opening the 12-mile section to Redmire, thus linking into the currently freight-only route to Northallerton. The indomitable Ruth Annison is very much behind the venture and also ultimately hopes that local interest and backing will see the 6-mile gap to the west and Garsdale completing a memorable 'Beeching turnabout' for this dale.

REDMIRE: The current terminus of the Wensleydale branch is at Redmire. In 1950, four years before the end of the branch passenger service, Class 'G5' No 67314 (Northallerton MPD) pulls away from the Station Master, left holding the disposed section token. The train is the 14.03 from Northallerton and has taken 1 hour 7 minutes to reach Redmire, due to terminate at Hawes at 15.35 – certainly leisurely stuff! Even in 1950 Redmire has that run-down look with sad holiday posters looking more a parody of earlier happier times before mass motor cars. *JWA*

Today, in June 1989, the platform has been curtailed to accommodate the extended headshunt (the buffer stop is just visible to the extreme left). Surprisingly the long sleepers for the catch point rails still lie amongst the creeping weeds. The shape on the gable end shows where the former outbuildings once were. The station house is now much simplified but retains the characteristic massive chimneys. Appropriately, just arriving with the limestone empties from Redcar BSC are *Wensleydale* and *Leyburn*, Class '37s' Nos 37667 and 37668 respectively. *ART*

Richmond Branch

CROFT SPA: Two Class 'A8' 4-6-2T engines greet each other on up and down Richmond workings at Croft Spa on the main line south of Darlington. What an amazingly peaceful setting considering that even as these branch trains come to a gentle halt there are several ECML expresses pounding down upon the location to bypass the village station without a nod in acknowledgement! The Richmond description on pages 44-45 more thoroughly describes branch motive power. As for the station, already by the late 'fifties it was no longer considered a justifiable delay point for ECML services, so intending main-station passengers had to travel to Darlington to make connections. *JWA*

Today the outline of the prominent tree is still vaguely discernible, but little else reveals the secret of the site. The main station building is represented by a lone signalling location box and the undoubted care of the Station Master, seen in the earlier view, counts for nought when momentarily glimpsed from a speeding Intercity 125 on an Edinburgh–King's Cross through train in March 1990. *ART*

ERYHOLME JUNCTION (or DALTON): South of Croft Spa on the 44 miles built between York and Darlington in 1841 by the Great North of England Railway, Eryholme (previously known as Dalton) came with the construction of the Richmond branch in 1846 and, together with Pilmoor, had no road access as it simply served to make connections between two routes. The station buildings were in the 'V' of the junction serving both directions and our older view shows the branch platforms on a curve off the ECML to enable clearance and better regulation of trains from the Richmond direction. Renaming to 'Eryholme' took place in 1901, closure coming ten years later when Croft Spa became the interchange point. *JWA*

In February 1989 we were amazed to find an entire platform edge leading a claustrophobic existence amid advancing nature a mere stone's throw from ECML expresses. A solitary station concrete lamp post has survived because of its being valueless?). *KG*

Eryholme seems traditionally to have been at the forefront of experimentation into signalling methods and was at the limit of the first main-line section to see a form of automatic colour lights (1928) preceded by Raven-installed AWS, operated by engine contact brushes upon energised ramps and installed in 1911-12. The old signal box (above) now forms a spectre against the horizon of new technology and alone marks the spot where Richmond passengers once awaited their ECML connections. *KG*

WALKERVILLE: The Catterick Military Railway was connected to the Richmond branch by the junction at Catterick Bridge. In 1950 Class 'L1' 2-6-4T No 67750 negotiates an open level crossing. *JWA*

In 1989 there is no trace of the crossing, and considerably more road traffic – Alan Thompson played safe and stayed on the verge! He was informed that the building visible in the background of both views was called the 'Pink Palace' by the Green Howards! *ART*

The military presence is well to the fore as an 'A5'-hauled train is flagged across the same crossing approximately ten years later. *JWA*

CATTERICK CAMP HALT: The old Camp Halt was revisited by an RCTS special on 11 October 1952 with Class 'A5' No 69842 at the head. A present-day equivalent was impossible because of dense undergrowth and saplings. *JWA*

RICHMOND: One of the 13 Hawthorn, Leslie & Co Class 'A5/2' engines, built during 1925 for the North Eastern area of the LNER (although based on Robinson's GC design as introduced at Gorton Works in 1911), stands at Richmond awaiting departure time. Large strong tank engines with caged bunkers, they were delivered new to the Newcastle area sheds until 1928 when many moved to Saltburn to replace ageing Class 'H1' engines on the Darlington turns. By 1939 the entire 13 had congregated on Darlington MPD and for the next six war years they did valiant service on the branches radiating from there, especially to Richmond, where few servicemen at Catterick Camp could forget them – especially when being carried away homeward on leave! By July 1952 No 69837 was to be found working out its life at Hull where she worked for many years hauling the heavy workmen's trains to the aircraft factory at Brough. All 13 were withdrawn in 1958 – victims of diesel railcars – and No 69837 was the last to go, in December, after 33 years of excellent service. *JWA*

It was welcome to find that in May 1989 the station was in use as a garden centre, the ornate trimmings of this now listed structure well maintained. The station was designed by G. T. Andrews to GNER orders in 1845-6, and is special in having twin spans with light wrought iron trusses finished in the Gothic character of the day and highly decorative timberwork gables set with small panelled windows. The River Swale bridge separating the station from the town, built at the same time as the station, unusually carried Y&NR bridge number plates (No 8) although it carried no track! *ART*

Richmond was chosen by Major General Franklyn, GOC Catterick Division and Colonel of the Regiment, to mark the 250th anniversary of the raising of the Regiment (in 1688) by naming Class 'V2' No 4806 (later 60835) *The Green Howard* at the ceremony shown above on 24 September 1938, and displaying the station's internal character to good advantage. *BR*

Rails to Harrogate

COPGROVE: On the penultimate day of working, 21 September 1950, Class 'G5' 0-4-4T No 67337 is sadly greeted as one of the last few remaining arrivals at Copgrove with, on this occasion, the 17.00 Harrogate to Pilmoor push-pull service. The engineers' recovery wagons stand ghoulishly awaiting their task! At the same time as Copgrove's demise, freight facilities were withdrawn on the Brafferton–Pilmoor section, leaving only the stretch between Knaresborough and Brafferton to survive as freight only until October 1964. No 67337 was a Starbeck (50D) engine at this time, and was cut up at Darlington Works in April 1957 after 56 years' service in the district. *J. W Hague/JWA Collection*

We visited the same spot on 28 June 1989. It can be seen that it is yet another very pleasantly renovated private residence with a particularly fine lawn covering what proved to be the not so 'permanent' way. We wish to record our thanks to the property owners who graciously allowed our visit to interrupt their teatime. *ART*

KNARESBOROUGH VIADUCT: Railways penetrated Knaresborough on 30 October 1848 at Hay Park temporary station, courtesy of the unlikely named East & West Yorkshire Junction Railway Co (later merged into George Hudson's York & North Midland). Through running between Harrogate and York was delayed for three years by the collapse of the first viaduct at this point; the Leeds & Thirsk Railway's (finally agreed) design incorporated a castellated look to achieve aesthetic harmony for the new planning-conscience town fathers. The final construction, seen here, is the pleasing result. On 30 April 1949 Class 'D20' No 62375 leads its train over the River Nidd with a returning Leeds train, while off-duty National Servicemen mill around looking forward to some boating activity on the bank opposite the path leading to Mother Shipton's cave complex. *JWA*

The social habits of today haven't changed so very much if this 40-year 'time warp' can be believed – but canoes as a means of pleasure have definitely waned! *ART*

KNARESBOROUGH STATION: The view from the station to the south-west is across the viaduct; the signalmen in the curious turret-shaped gable-end cabin have an excellent view, whilst to their left they keep an eye on the passengers and traffic at the crossing. The 30 April 1949 view is typical of that era, showing a railway starved of investment cash following the war and with certainly very little money to spare for grooming permanent way back to pre-Second World War standards. The 'D20s' were introduced in the last year of the 19th century and it is quite remarkable that they survived well into the 1950s, remaining a favourite of enginemen to the last. No 62375, shown here hauling a Harrogate–York train, appears elsewhere in this book and became one of the last six based on Alnmouth — all withdrawn during 1957. *JWA*

In the red and cream livery of West Yorkshire PTE sponsorship, a Class '144' 'Metro Train' brings in a midday Leeds–Knaresborough terminating service. Note how the shunting signal is protected from wayward motorists. Now publicised as the 'Harrogate Line', BR distribute imaginative travel information to accompany a journey over the route telling us that the old station building is now a restaurant called 'Off the Rails', and well worth a visit! *ART*

HARROGATE STRAY: The Stray – 200 acres of greensward – virtually surrounds the town centre and was the sight of Harrogate's first railway station. A stone commemorates the fact and was laid in 1949 near the Prince of Wales Hotel: it reads 'Site of Brunswick Station of the York and N Midland railway. Opened 20th July 1848, closed 1st August 1862'. The Stray's excellent facilities for train watching must have bred many generations of spotters and, as can be seen, the perimeter was also utilised for garden allotments on both sides of the track (could this have been a perk of NER employment?). Seen here in 1953, the well-appointed 'CTAC Scottish Tour Express' is inward-bound behind Gresley 'Pacific' No 60084 *Trigo*, a Leeds Neville Hill stalwart that was eventually withdrawn in November 1964 after 14 years at that shed serving the area's travelling public. *JWA*

Forty years of unfettered tree growth from the richly cultivated garden strip has robbed us of much in the way of reference points beyond the immediate railway. BREL Derby/Leyland 1984-built Class '141' railbus (in West Yorkshire red/cream livery) sets out across the Stray in July 1990 with a Knaresborough–Leeds service, the foliage enforcing a more square-on viewpoint for today's comparison. *ART*

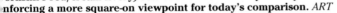

Harrogate – northern capital of Victorian splendour, lavish parks, beautiful gardens and cosmopolitan charm. The present-day Harrogate also wants to be known for its modern International Conference and Exhibition centre. However, the station currently badly fails to mirror much of what is to be found beyond its walls, explained perhaps by the fact that it has regularly been a pawn not only between planners' aspirations but also the two different sides of the town it manages to neatly dissect. It is currently again the subject of much discussion and the emotive subject of a station 'through' development linking the town's split sites has again raised its head.

On 9 November 1990 the *Yorkshire Evening Post* carried the story about Harrogate station proposals commenting that BR had attacked a radical new transport scheme on the grounds that it would 'jeopardise the town's vital rail links'. This comment by BR was aimed at draft plans showing a new-style Harrogate station acting as a new 'via media' between the two parts of the town split by the railways, but creating a barrier across the through route forcing train services from either direction to terminate!

Four months later another storm erupted when North Yorkshire councillors accused BR of being 'mean' by not contributing anything to a proposed new station at Hornbeam Park, planned to serve a nearby business estate and Harrogate College of Arts and Technology. BR replied that 'while we are not prepared to contribute . . . we will meet maintenance costs once [the new station] is operational . . . .' The latest news before going to press was on 26 April 1991 when the *Harrogate Advertiser* announced 'Full steam ahead at Hornbeam', adding: 'The new rail halt . . . could be open by October next year after county chiefs agreed to pay £150,000 towards the project . . . The district council will be discussing with British Rail the possibility of resiting Starbeck Station in conjunction with the Taylor Woodrow development and providing an additional station to the East of Knaresbrorough.'

Harrogate Council, North Yorkshire County Council and British Rail, having thus ironed out their differences, have entered the 'nineties in a most positive way to solve the horrendous traffic problems currently occurring in this area and are even now looking at further station developments plus park/ride incentives. Harrogate is grasping the transport nettle in a way which confirms that the age of the train really will be in the 21st century.

HARROGATE STATION (1): Until 1862 passengers going to, say, Wetherby, Tadcaster or Church Fenton left from the earlier Brunswick station at the 'Stray', while the Leeds & Thirsk Railway kept to the east of the town and used Starbeck station as a busy interchange point. The building of the Central station, in 1862, seen here, allowed the other, York & North Midland, station to close. The newer station changed little over the years until the first joint development scheme of 1965 brought about the nine-storey Copthall Tower and the smaller Bridge House office block, built across the tracks and shown on page 52. Our 8 June 1958 view records ex-LMS 'Crab' 2-6-0 No 42770 arriving with train 'N566', a Guiseley–Scarborough additional. *T. J. Edgington*

In June 1990 the two remaining reference points are the station house chimneys (proving a stark contrast against the Copthall Tower backcloth!) and the back wall end-support column (just visible in the earlier view). The retained middle road acts as overnight standage for units left for Harrogate train crews, and the north-end bay, once used for the now abandoned Leeds Northern route to the north (see page 56ff) provides a much-needed car park amid somewhat bare amenities. *KG*

HARROGATE STATION (2): Again seen on 8 June 1958 a 'cat's whisker' Craven-built DMU enters Harrogate from the Leeds direction with the RCTS 'Roses' railtour from Manchester Victoria. Across in the south-end bay, a Fowler tank backs on to through Bradford coaches and another relatively new DMU lurks in the shadows beyond with a Leeds City service. *T. J. Edgington*

The viewpoint in June 1990 can be seen to be about 40 yards nearer the main station area than the older view. This change is due to the bridge being widened (towards the camera) to accommodate the three-storey Bridge House office block that eclipsed the old Leeds & Holbeck Building Society office in the mid 'sixties. The 1990 comparison isn't favourable towards rail activity; although the bay is still evident it is now an empty void. Two unusual floor-mounted three-aspect signals stand guard as a narrow-bodied Leyland Class '141' comes in with a Leeds–York through service. *KG*

HARROGATE, DRAGON JUNCTION: Straight ahead is the main Leeds Northern line which crossed below the ECML route at Northallerton, arriving here by way of Melmerby, Ripon and Bilton Junction (see page 56ff) where the choice was straight on for Starbeck, avoiding Harrogate, or right to Dragon Junction and this location (the line from Starbeck can be seen trailing in from the east). A favourite location for spotters and photographers, this triangle of junctions is set in pleasant rolling countryside and our 1951 view depicts a star performer on the route in the shape of Neville Hill depot's well-maintained Class 'A3' No 60036 *Colombo* leading a 'blood and spilt milk' set on a Newcastle–Liverpool 'flyer'. *JWA*

The sparse population (discounting the city of Ripon) along the Leeds Northern route was its undoing; closure to passenger trains ended through working on this more direct Leeds route in March 1967. On 22 July 1989 a most profound alteration can thus be seen, whereby the main-line route has been the one to completely disappear leaving the branch from York to sweep into view past the remaining siding alongside C. K. Raws factory. It might be said that the Dragon now lies dead as railcar No 141117 rattles towards Harrogate over now simple trackwork. *ART*

STARBECK: Making a welcome change to the prolific (and easier to locate) 'past' passenger train views is this quite rare study of the once numerous 'J77' Class designed by Wilson Worsdell and introduced in 1899. Twenty survived into 1957; the last, going in February 1961, was No 68408. Our Starbeck MPD example, No 68393, was one of five allocated here mainly for shunting and, as seen, occasionally for medium-size short-trip haulage. This train must certainly constitute a medium to heavy haul for this little 0-6-0 as it appears to have a good sprinkling of heavily loaded vehicles amongst the empties. Behind the engine is a BK container used for household removals, two benzine tanks and two others which are just about to be deposited into the MOD sidings behind, in exchange for the two empties at the discharge area. The picture is thought to date from 1951 and displays much detail typical of the immediate post-Second World War period with many anonymous MOD fuelling points dotted intermittently across the Vale of York. *JWA Trust Collection*

The area, now heavily fenced and possibly recovering from fuel contamination, lies idle, the majority of passengers on this Leeds to York railcar oblivious to the part this Starbeck field contributed to the war effort of '39-'45. *ART*

THORP ARCH: Newport (51B) engine No 90461 is taking the slower (but planned) way around from Cleveland to the Midlands line via Church Fenton with Tees-side semi-finished steel products for the 'master cutlers' of Sheffield, and is seen trundling south through Thorp Arch (between Wetherby racecourse and Newton Kyme). The station is caught as a 'still life' reflecting the character of the early 'fifties with a 'palvan' in the goods siding and a beckoning 'Come to Sunny Bridlington' poster alongside two standard LNER fire buckets! Originally 'Thorp Arch for Boston Spa' (1 mile distant), it was renamed as shown in June 1961, just a few years before closure in January 1964. *JWA*

We caught extensive modernisation in hand when visiting in June 1989, perhaps just in time to witness a remarkable transformation about to occur. Restoration of the original timber spandrels and roof supports is well under way but which readers have noticed the clever extension adjacent to the chimney breast – how well it fits into the scheme of things! Also of note is the goods shed, surely worthy of 'listing' and still with its smoke smudge above the elliptical cut-out curve. The lady proprietor can be seen getting to grips with the lawned area which 28 years earlier would have been in the '4 foot' on the approach line to Church Fenton. We thank her for permission to record the current situation. *ART*

Leeds Northern and branches

ARTHINGTON, between Leeds and Harrogate, and just north of Bramhope Tunnel, had just two stations; the first, opened in 1849, was resited in 1865 due to its original position (alongside the Harewood–Pool road) being somewhat inconvenient as a junction interchange station with the newly constructed branch off to the west and Ilkley. The temporary 1865 construction was eventually given 'permanent' facilities during 1876; further rebuilding then followed in 1896, resulting in the visually rather poor brick-built affair seen in this 30 August 1952 view showing a Class 'G5' 0-4-4T No 67274 calling in at the south-west platform of the triangular group hauling a Leeds to Ilkley train. *JWA*

Closed completely by March 1965, the two concrete station nameboard supports remain as a pointless exercise eventually to become strangled by creeping weeds and presumably lost forever, the final tangible evidence of triangular Arthington. *ART*

PATELEY BRIDGE: The 1862 Nidd Valley branch lay between Harrogate and the place illustrated — Pateley Bridge — diverging from the Leeds Northern main line at Ripley Junction, a few miles north of the River Nidd viaduct near Bilton. There were five intermediate stations before reaching here and almost 2 miles further on lay Wath, where a Light Railway Order paved the way beyond, first to Ramsgill, then Lofthouse for access to the Bradford Corporation reservoir construction sites at Angram. The light railway carried a passenger service from 1907 and even though its route trailed into Pateley Bridge, very close to the two-platform terminal, passengers still had to walk to bridge the gap! The light railway closed to passengers and most goods traffic on the last day of 1929, and Pateley Bridge became the official railhead of the valley. The branch staggered on to its final day, 2 April 1951, seen here with a 'J39' on the freight pick-up whilst Class 'G5' No 67253 has the ignominious task of bringing passenger services to a close on a day that saw over an inch of rain in a very short time. The goods pick-up continued until 1964. *JWA*

In September 1989, only the inhabitants of the station house can remember the branch in its heyday — it is an old people's home! *ART*

Rail revival in the **Ripon** area took a major step forward with the formation of the Harrogate, Ripon & Northallerton Railway Company during 1989, now the Ripon Rail Reinstatement Association (RRRA). The line, closed by October 1969, was formerly the chosen passenger route of what today would be loosely termed 'North Transpennine' and, prior to 1959, also accommodated all ECML slower freight trains (ie classes 7 to 9), bound for the Midlands.

An extraordinary fact to come out of the caption research was that during its last full year of passenger operations – 1966 – this section lost a paltry £12,500! More investigations revealed that in spite of strong opposition to closure, no first-option, cost-cutting economy options such as singling of the route and unstaffing of stations, etc, were first attempted (as took place eventually to save the Harrogate–York route). The line was therefore allowed to die, in the way that was certainly peculiar if not downright obscene! Certainly almost everyone in those less environmentally friendly times assumed it was a case of 'RIP Ripon'!

Today, inital examination of the scenario to reopen has suggested a £15 million minimum target; this fact, backed by the proposed radical Conservative Railfreight revival policy plus an increase in the population (expected to be in excess of 40,000 by 1995) seems to suggest an answer to the prayers of the many caught up in the growing scourge of this district today — snarled-up, jam-packed highways.

The examination, carried out in 1988, found 90 per cent of the trackbed intact and the Nidd Viaduct in fairly good condition. However, south of Ripon, at Littlethorpe, the line is lost for some distance under a small estate. Of the remaining obstacles, as the photos opposite illustate, perhaps the costliest engineering item of rail revival is the lost viaduct across central Ripon.

Other planned stations in the reinstatement scheme include Pickhill, Melmerby, Ripon racecourse and Bilton (on the outskirts of Harrogate).

If the rail scheme fails, NYCC are planning to use part of the existing trackbed for a Ripon bypass – this was once a very familiar story to most readers but is certainly contrary to today's enlightened thinking and a reversal of the current transport policies of Yorkshire generally. Time alone will tell how Ripon will grasp this particular nettle!

RIPON (1): This summer 1953 picture has caught aged Class 'D20' No 62387 (seen also at Alne on page 79 just before withdrawal) assisting one of the troublesome Class 'A2/2' engines in the form of No 60501 *Cock o' the North* (built as a Class 'P2' in 1934). From the concern showing on both sets of crews' faces, it seems very likely that they may have had to set back with a heavier-than-normal Newcastle–Liverpool load, and are anxiously awaiting hand-signals from the station staff. *J. W. Hague/Courtesy of D. Tyreman Collection*

Replacement today of the missing viaduct at current costs would most probably take up a large chunk of the £15 million RRRA budget. In the meantime, and having gained new access from the missing supports, the since re-roofed garage proprietor must wonder if he is again to to be cast into darkness. *ART*

RIPON (2): Pulling away from Ripon on a dull winter afternoon in the early 'fifties is train 917, and gauging by the motley collection of vintage vehicles in tow it is an excursion 'scratch' set returning to the NER area. A key city in the route of the Leeds Northern Railway Company, Ripon and its accompanying 25 villages (within a 6-mile radius) were contributing just under 90,000 passengers a year by the turn of the century. It is now hard to believe that (from 1902) Ripon was also served by through trains to King's Cross! *D. Tyreman Collection*

Alan Thompson took this picture on 3 April 1991 (in the nick of time) from the foundations of a partially built house! In view of the built-on 'permanent way' in the station area, any rail revival project here is completely out of the question. Fortunately, the new company would be using these circumstances to redirect a new route nearer the densest population areas. The well-preserved and maintained station alone survives. *ART*

MELMERBY: An Act in 1865 gave the NER powers to connect with the MR's Settle & Carlisle route at Hawes via the Ure Valley from the Leeds Northern at Melmerby. However, the already complete Northallerton to Leyburn section was the natural way to the west; the scheme, abandoned in 1869, meant that Tanfield and Masham were potentially forgotten rail locations. To appease them, the NER agreed to build a single-line branch to Masham, starting from Melmerby, and this opened in June 1875. With the branch already completed to the east, to Thirsk via Topcliffe, Melmerby became an unlikely railway focal point, considering its own population was then no more than 284! Opened in 1848, the station survived the initial Beeching axe to be eventually closed on 4 March 1967 (the branch goods train from Ripon to the army depot at Melmerby continued for a further two years). We see Melmerby at an auspicious time — Coronation Day, 1953 — as Leeds Neville Hill (50B) Class 'B1' No 61065 diverges to the east for Topcliffe and Thirsk on a Leeds–Northallerton working, passing the many Union Jacks fluttering in a strong easterly breeze. The main through route is between the engine and signal box, with the Masham branch out of sight to the right. *JWA*

A very hazy 1989 summer day shows that the site of the station is now engulfed amid feathery wild grass and beyond the now unimpeded road is the all too familiar road transport distribution depot filling the void left by rail's pull-out. *ART*

TOPCLIFFE: The Ripon–Thirsk section of the Leeds & Thirsk Railway contrived to break the hold that George Hudson had on Yorkshire–North East England traffic; the line was built over four years due to its complex engineering requirements and was up and running for both goods and passengers by 1 June 1848. This route preceded the Melmerby–Northallerton extension by four years and rather duplicated it except that Thirsk Junction station (with the GNE main line) provided rather more source traffic than the very rural Pickhill route to Northallerton. In the late 'fifties *The Atherstone*, a 'D49' Class engine, heads east past the signal box, bathed in sunlight, with a Sunday diverted Leeds–Newcastle express. *JWA*

The hazards of standing in nondescript places and casually taking pictures of parked cars and a spreading tree would appear on the face of it slight. Alan Thompson, however, hadn't reckoned on a sharp-eyed sentry on duty at the Albemarle Barracks (behind the camera), noting his car registration number. He took the photograph whilst heading south on holiday and was mystified when contacted from his home in the North East asking that he contact the nearest police station urgently. When he did he was given the third degree treatment until he produced the picture of *The Atherstone* and further evidence of similar research. The film was ultimately returned, and here is the offending view. The tree now marks the signal box position 30 years (almost to the day) after closure, on 12 September 1959. Our thanks to the occupants of the station house. *ART*

1 spite of its established presence on both the Intercity and Regional Railways maps, **Jorthallerton** looks likely to be the focal point of yet two more passenger sources om the westward — if their respective scheme campaigns maintain momentum vithin the even more enlightened transport times in which we now live. One set of romoters would like to see Wensleydale opened up again to travellers and eventually onnect into the lucrative Settle & Carlisle market (see pages 36-7). To the south-west, ut without existing infrastructure, is the Ripon Railway Reinstatement Association see page 58), currently being assessed for viability by railway reinstatement onsultant Scott Handley (we should hopefully know, by publication date, the utcome). These two routes, with the advantage of privatisation, would expect a fair rack of the free enterprise whip and thus a share of the running rights into and hrough Northallerton – an interesting thought, but jumping the gun some way yet!

The 1841 main line of the Great North of England Railway was bisected at Jorthallerton in 1852 by the Leeds & Thirsk (later Leeds Northern) Railway from Melmerby towards Stockton; a subsequent additional northern bay was provided at he main station for Hawes branch trains and one at the south for those starting here or Harrogate and Leeds.

From 1901 up to about 1942 all neighbouring locations on the ECML were onstantly in a transient state due to the ever improving main-line streamlining. Iowever, Northallerton station, southbound side, surprisingly remained virtually naltered from its 1841 shape until the early 1980s when the final awnings where emoved. The northbound (downside) platform was radically changed in 1911, ecoming an island to accommodate today's equivalent of North Transpennine ervices, otherwise causing delays. Also at the northern end, but at the lower level of he Leeds Northern route, was the engine shed, the coal depots and locomotive urntable being up above near the station approach on the opposite side.

Although the Leeds Northern route crossed below the East Coast route in 1852, nterchange facilities where not built until 1856 when the curve joining the two routes vas commissioned and the old Leeds Northern station to the north closed. Further dditions were an annexed low-level platform to accommodate trains from the Ripon ne, followed in 1901 by a connection (Cordio) to allows those same services into the nain station. (More about the low-level facilities, including the loco shed, will be ound in Part 2.)

The now out of use slow line platforms were updated in 1941 and served for dditional troop interchange in this, the centre of training camp country, remained hereafter for some time for use during weekend diversion work.

Regular passenger services over the direct LN route from Middlesbrough waned luring the 1960s, but the route is again in contention with, in July 1991, an Intercity 25 train again routed this way – albeit Sundays only at present – following the demise of the 'Cleveland Executive' in 1990.

Northallerton it seems is coming out of a questionable time and into an electric era s surely befits the county town and HQ of the North Yorkshire County Council, as an be seen in the following photographs.

NORTHALLERTON (1): Appropriately seen arriving on 18 September 1954 with the 11 am from Saltburn is Northallerton's own Class 'D20' No 62347 and revealing a very determined-looking driver remaining loyal to his NER cap badge six years after nationalisation. One of four 51J 'D20' engines at this time (others were 62359, 62388 and 62391), this is a particularly good study of an NER engine in post-war conditions with 'slam door' wooden-bodied stock on leisurely timings. The cattle dock is accommodating a raft of pigeon vans and looks as if it may have recently been 'faced' and upgraded in height. Northallerton's loco shed closed in March 1963, the remaining engines transferring to Darlington MPD. *J. W. Hague/Courtesy of Dave Tyreman Collection*

The first forward leap in time, to 1989, allows a more detailed look into the tightly curving yard, and it is perhaps a surprise to find that the electrical engineer has taken the overhead 'knitting' around to the buffer stops! The platform starting signal remains unchanged and is still described as N (Northallerton) 54; however, it was awaiting change of ownership into York signalling territory at any time and Northallerton signal box was demolished when the transition took place during Easter that year. *ART*

We had no option but to show another update due to the now rapidly changing ECML, and in April 1991 the handsome signal box is no more, the small yard is emptier but tidier and the colour light is now described as N (York) 467. The double junction beyond to the Stockton direction is now clearly seen and the Intercity 125 on the London run is replaced by a brand new Liverpool-bound Class '158' which, in years before, would probably have been routed to Leeds via Harrogate along the Leeds Northern main line. *ART*

NORTHALLERTON (2): A little further south, on the 1911 altered northbound (downside) platform in the summer of 1949, John Armstrong's viewpoint gives the observer a glimpse of the 1841 GNE railway architecture that existed up to the early 1980s, when the awnings and support columns finally disappeared. It would have been a sad omission if we had failed to show the crack train of the Leeds Northern route, so here it is. The engine, Gresley 'Pacific' No 60074 *Harvester*, was particularly interesting at this time as she was one of the seven of her class tried in the experimental purple livery at the time of nationalisation, and readers will have to take our word for the fact that she is seen here in this odd colour! *Harvester* became BR blue in November 1950, conforming with her many sisters. She is about to take the route via Ripon and Harrogate to Leeds and then King's Cross with the famous 'Queen of Scots' Pullman. *JWA*

The current viewpoint in April 1991 shows the 'bus shelter' facilities of the northbound side, the now energised OHLE, and the current style 'leg-up' step below the upside platform for station staff unable to use the subway. Red Parcels-liveried Class '47' No 47476 of the RXLC Crewe Pool hurries train 1V64 south to York and ultimately Plymouth with the midday postal from Newcastle-upon-Tyne. *ART*

East Coast Main Line north of York

CROFT VIADUCT: Sweeping effortlessly across the boundary from Durham into Yorkshire is Gateshead Class 'A3' No 60060 *The Tetrarch* with a Newcastle–Liverpool express in the early 1950s. *JWA*

If you look carefully at today's scene the 'YORKSHIRE' sign is just visible, but much else has changed during the intervening 40 years of indiscriminate shrub and tree growth. The view is no longer an attractive possibility for modern-day photographers – especially as we now have a small sewage plant in the foreground. An Intercity 125 is seen heading south for King's Cross in February 1990. *ART*

WISKE MOOR: Wiske takes its name from the river of the same name which meanders hence from its source near Swainby. It once had a station — Danby Wiske — which served a small surrounding population (418 people in 1901) from 1884 until closure in 1958. But more interesting for us, comparing these three views spanning 50 years, is the evolution of the track layout. The widening scheme of 1933 resulted in our first view, whilst the scheme of 1942 greeted the 'Deltic' era. Finally we see the modifications associated with the preparations for the July 1991 ECML 'switch-on'.

We found that Wiske Moor was a favourite location of John Armstrong, thus making final selection difficult; at decision time it was something different that caught our eyes. We therefore hope that readers will find the sight of a lowly Class 'J39' 0-6-0 mixed traffic engine hauling south coast stock on a down Bournemouth–Newcastle express a welcome change from the everyday sight of a sleek silver express. *JWA*

From 1939 we go forward to the summer of 1964 and the then common sight of a green/yellow 'Deltic' taking water for its Stones train heating boiler, an occurrence not generally associated with diesel-electric locomotives! It can be seen that the 1942 alterations resulted in a reprofiled down slow line beneath a new single-span bridge. *JWA*

The period to March 1990 has witnessed the disappearance of the troughs and the removal of both slow lines, but now with additional versatility of bi-directional running and signalling, Intercity 125 power car 43094 leads the 10 am King's Cross–Edinburgh express over the site of the steam-age troughs. *ART*

NORTHALLERTON SOUTH: We are now back at Northallerton, where John Armstrong lived for many years. His particular favourite viewing location, at the south end of the downside platform, meant another difficult choice from the many photographs he took here over an approximate ten-year period. We eventually chose this foursome from the point of view of location alteration, and as a summary of 40 years of motive power transition.

In the first, 1948, photograph, Thompson Class 'B1' No E1289 (later 61289) is still a relatively new engine and is painted in the lined apple-green livery of the LNER but now with the recent addition of 'British Railways' spelt out fully over the tender side. The train is mainly formed of 'highfits' and appears to have come from York Yards with a Class 'H' goods for Forth Junction. *JWA*

The next view, assumed to be about 1970, is a quite rare picture of the prototype Intercity 125 and Mark I front end design showing its mettle over the Plain of York 'racetrack' whilst on proving trials. *JWA*

On comparison with the view of 1989 and a production Intercity 125 set, the prototype's windows appear to be like portholes. By now, the down slow line (outer face) facilities have gone, returning Northallerton to the pre-1911 situation, when there were complaints that down 'flyers' were often baulked by dilatory stopping services. *ART*

Two years on and perhaps the final radical alterations have been made to the down side as we see the latest form of Regional Railway 'Express' North Transpennine service in the shape of a Class '158' set about to call with the mid-afternoon Leeds–Darlington service. The platform extension for the larger electric train sets has completely hidden the underbridge support girder, and the greatest aid to the operators' flexibility is seen in the form of bi-directional signalling with signal Y476 at the end of the now two-way platform. The fencing isn't quite complete, but that hardly justifies a fifth view! *ART*

71

THIRSK NORTH: Of particular interest to students of signalling equipment are these views at the north end of Thirsk station. The Thirsk area seems always to have been in the vanguard of signalling changes, and as far back as 1905 was the northern extremity of experimental gas-operated semaphore signalling extending from Alne, which remained in use for this high-speed section until the early use of colour lights here in 1933. These early and simple forms of colour lights showed only two aspects — red and green for the stop signal and yellow and green for the distant. Gresley 'Pacific' No 4900 *Gannet* is about to pass through Thirsk at the head of the up 'Flying Scotsman' wearing a coat of garter blue and hauling teak brown coaches in 1939. The not inconsiderable Thirsk down sidings are evident over to the left, whilst two water columns and bag-warming equipment add even more to the rich periphery of this pre-war setting. *JWA*

Fifty years on – almost to the day – sees the latest four- aspect signalling equipment and the now obsolete Thirsk signal box lying abandoned in the distance. Still keeping the faith in wedge-front trains, today's Intercity 125s are themselves now giving way to Class '91' electrics on front-line ECML services. Thirsk's inner face platforms have now gone, but the old platelayers' hut plus the NER cast iron trespass notice maintain the continuity of this dynamic location. *ART*

THIRSK SOUTH: Two scenes depicting typical up traffic on this portion of the ECML at Thirsk in 1939. John Armstrong's first view shows a Gresley Class 'A8', a rebuild of a Raven NER Class 'D', blowing off vigorously as it pulls out of the up main platform with a Darlington–Leeds express. Later in the day Raven Class 'B16' 4-6-0 No 920 comes off the two-track section and takes the slow line, bound, it seems, for one of the inter-company freight transfer yards in the Milford–Normanton area. It would be interesting to see the complete train consist – this tantalising glimpse reveals a fascinating mix! *Both JWA*

The intervening 50 years have seen many changes at Thirsk, not least the extension of the four tracks north to Northallerton (as a wartime necessity) with the subsequent addition of the outside face platforms. Today these platforms are all that remains as the station is no longer funded for main-line use and the inner face platforms have been cut back to allow line speed to be maintained. The scene on 29 June 1989 shows No 47488 *Rail Riders* pulling away from Thirsk with a Newcastle–Liverpool 'North Transpennine' service. Incredibly the bridge abutment remains as one significant point of reference. *ART*

The additional photograph shows the view in the opposite direction with a DMU bound for Leeds moving off along the branch to Topcliffe in about 1957. The engine shed which stands inside the junction lay derelict from closure in 1930 until demolition in 1965. *JWA*

40

PILMOOR: Six miles south of Thirsk and 16 miles north of York in the vale as flat as a pancake, Pilmoor was nevertheless interesting for its diverging branches. Coming off the Gilling branch with a Scarborough–Newcastle summer Saturday train in 1952, resplendent Heaton 'V2' Class locomotive No 60945 weaves across all four tracks to reach the down slow. Clearly visible are the two embankments (see opposite) and the comparatively new signal box, a result of the final ECML widening scheme here just ten years previously. *JWA*

Thirty-seven years on, the signal box is still extant but boarded up, the embankments are becoming wooded and relay cabins hyphenate the down slow. Few if any passengers on this Poole–Edinburgh service on 29 June 1989 will realise that Pilmoor had a station besides being a once busy cross-country junction! *ART*

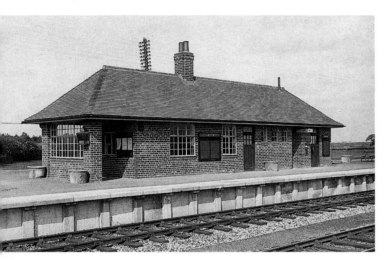

Seen shortly after completion in September 1937, Pilmoor's station building is a fine example of architectural modesty using the best materials of the day. Unfortunately no trace of it remains today. *BR*

'Where did four home signals stand on the East Coast Main Line, always completely ignored by passing trains?' This was a common enough quiz question at enginemen's mutual improvement classes in the NER area, and the answer (of course) was Pilmoor and the situation as illustrated. It is believed that these eyesight testing 'dummy' signals were constructed upon the old embankment designed to carry the branch from Harrogate over the ECML to Gilling (forming a fast Leeds–Scarborough route) which would avoid the Skelton Bridge 'throat'. The embankment and the bridge were indeed used, not for standard gauge trains, but for a narrow gauge railway used in tipping spoil from the 1933 ECML route-widening scheme. The next ECML improvement in 1942 saw the temporary bridge abolished, and the approach embankment – seen here – remained as one of the few hills on the flat vale, becoming an ideal mount for eyesight testing signals to be viewed by locomen from a distance.

The small wooden hut at the base seems to have been in communication with the accompanying testing inspector and was complete with a ground frame.

When looking through old locomen's histories, the item 'failed Pilmoor, reduced in grade' was a brief but sobering statement that for many meant the end of their career dream, ie attaining the 'Top Link' and becoming Kings of the Road! *JWA*

ALNE (1): This view from the platform shows touches of the Great North of England Railway construction work dating back to 1841. It can be seen that the arch on the up side allows the Easingwold branch Class 'J72' access to the outer face of the platform, while to our left, and out of sight, is an arch allowing entry to the goods yard. The Easingwold Railway is by now, 2 June 1957, freight only, and the branch guard has rather fine accommodation for his parcels. *JWA*

The brick bridge went in the 1959 final phase of ECML streamlining. In June 1989, two years before the 'switch-on', the midday Newcastle–Plymouth premium parcels express speeds south under the wires. *ART*

ALNE (2) looking south on 2 June 1957, and it can be seen that the old downside station building was a square, solid-looking boxy structure and linking the two platforms was a standard cast iron footbridge. A trim pedestrian gangway construction leads the public (and perhaps staff) from the Railway Hotel prominent in the right background behind the neat goods yard with its loading dock. To complete the picture what better than a NER Class 'R' back upon its old stamping ground where the class once regularly swept past working the fastest scheduled trains in the Empire. No 62387 was one of the last six of this class (later 'D20') which finally saw out their days on the Newcastle–Alnmouth service in 1955-57, except as here when they were specially requested to haul a Branch Line Society excursion throughout the Ryedale and Mowbray areas. No 62387 had but three months of active service remaining. *JWA*

On 29 June 1989 No 56129 motors past the site with an empty MGR coal train for the North East. The small goods shed remains, but little else. *ART*

Although 14th-century **York** was second only in importance to London, decline set in when traders began to bypass York for the larger and rapidly growing surrounding towns. York was paying heavily for the absence of minerals in its immediate area and mass depopulation was threatening when George Hudson was appointed as Chairman of the York & Midland Railway in the 1830s. Not only did he believe in York people but fought tooth and nail to prevent the Great North of England Railway from running south from Gateshead and diverting past York to link with other routes in the Tadcaster area. By doing this, Hudson virtually saved York from ignominy.

With York on the line, and at the convergence of many river routes, the station was guaranteed to become a great railway junction and York went from strength to strength. Workshops and large sidings associated with the railway sprang up everywhere outside the city walls and ironically the problem became one of overcrowding, with its side effect of social deprivation. There were about 900 back-to-back houses at the turn of the century when Seebohm Rowntree published his report on the serious conditions then prevailing in *Poverty – A Study of Town Life.*

He estimated that about 30 per cent of the population lived in poverty. His contribution to employment in his Rowntree's factory eventually challenged the numbers working for the NER and pushed the railway authorities to think in terms of better recreation and other facilities for its own large staff numbers.

Today the carriage works are privately owned, Clifton and Dringhouses yards are closed, and the freight business for the sidings and wagon works reduced. The main Eastern Region HQ buildings on each side of Station Rise plus the newer Hudson House have become the mainstay of employment. They are the focal points of new technology linked with railway operations rapidly moving into the 21st century computer networks and fault controls are based on York HQ, feeding out to all parts of the widespread area, formerly known as the Eastern Region.

From Monday 24 July 1991 York could no longer be called the Regional HQ resulting from the most radical shake-up in BR's organisational history since the days when Geddes and Butterworth revolutionised NER accountancy practices. From that date individual workers were to report to their respective Business Manager everyone having been categorised into a distinct business function.

This reorganisation, known to railway people as the Organisation for Quality (O-F-Q), finally ended the traditional geographical boundaries born of the 1923 Grouping, once supported by the mysterious workings of the Railway Clearing House. The traditional boundary with ScotRail on the ECML at Marshall Meadows, for instance, disappeared overnight, and InterCity managers at York now control financially the route to Edinburgh then via Carstairs to the buffer stops at Glasgow Central.

YORK CLIFTON (1): Northbound from York the railway swings to the left past Waterworks Junction (where the Scarborough line leaves) and skirts alongside the North shed wall until reaching this point where Clifton carriage sidings and the North shed holding sidings sandwiched the ECML. From the 1930s a feature of this section was the beautifully maintained ornamental border with a touch of simple topiary. We have John Miller, Chief Area Engineer, to thank. In June 1963, Class 'A3' 'Pacific' No 60066 *Merry Hampton*, then of King's Cross Top Shed, leaves York northbound with a Hull–Edinburgh (Saturdays) train made up of examples by Thompson, Gresley and BR. She is showing signs of neglect with an ash-burnt smokebox door and in fact survived in traffic only three more months, being withdrawn with six of her King's Cross sisters in September 1963. *ART*

Today's picture, taken in April 1991, confirms that the ornamental border died soon after. On the left, Clifton carriage sidings, newly modernised with a brand new electronic washing shed in 1984, only made a further three years' contribution and were closed down during 1987, a victim of the switch to diesel unit operation on the transpennine route network and the subsequent decision to maintain such units elsewhere. They have now been demolished. *KG*

YORK CLIFTON (2): March 1963 sees Class 'A1' 'Pacific' No 60156 *Great Central* of Doncaster Carr Loc comfortably lift nine standard BR coaches forming the King's Cross–Tyne Commissioners Quay (Percy Main) boa train. *ART*

The small bushes at this point failed to see their 30th birthday due to track remodelling near the North she junction. Over the expanse of wasteland that was once the North shed holding sidings, nothing today remains bu clinker mixed in with broken permanent way oddments. The 45 mph permanent speed restriction on the curv has been upped to 50 mph in recent years; York Minster continues to loom high on the horizon. *KG*

he National Railway Museum, opened in 1975 utilising the buildings of the old York
orth locomotive shed, is the second such museum to be established in the city, as
he photograph below illustrates.

Well visible to East Coast Main Line travellers, York North shed was a passing place
o look forward to with anticipation. There was always a chance of seeing LMS, GC or
E engines from distant-sounding locations following incursions to this city, the
lecca of tourism. From 1932 onwards, when the 'foreign visitors' shed at Queen
treet closed, the North shed was even more interesting.

Conceived in 1875 as a large 'L' shape, incorporating three adjoining roundhouses,
he shed opened in early 1878 and went through many stages of evolution as the
riginal turntable requirement crept up from 45 feet through 50 feet and 60 feet to the
932 application of a 70-foot Mundt electric turntable. That year also saw the
onstruction of a city landmark, the mechanical coaling plant, with its four chutes and
coal hopper capacity of 500 tons.

Exactly a decade later the North shed suffered much damage from a single German
omb and the subsequent rebuild became the North shed as known in latter steam
ays.

North shed closed officially to steam on 25 June 1967, but lingered on as a stabling
oint until 1973 when it closed completely pending renovation as the National
ailway Museum.

**HE OLD YORK MUSEUM: An historic occasion in York on 18 July 1947 was the opening of a railway-sponsored
useum on the site of the old Queen Street Works. The York Press Agency was commissioned by the LNER
ublicity Department to record some notable invited visitors, and seen here reviewing the collected engines, and
ne in particular very special in the hearts of Yorkshiremen (the Doncaster-built Stirling 'Single'), are, in the
entre, Mr C. M. Jenkins Jones CBE, once General Manager of the North Eastern area of the LNER, and two
irectors of the company, Mr Miles Beevor (left) and Sir Ronald Matthews.** *BR*

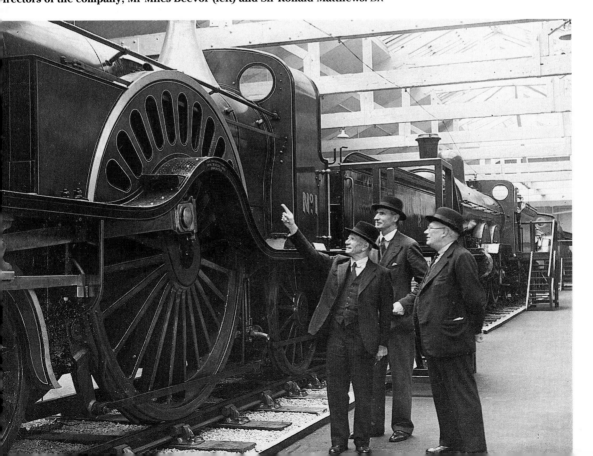

YORK NORTH SHED YARD (1): Our scene is typical of a 1963 visit to the depot during the years of diagramme[ ]ECML 'Pacific' power. Oddly reminiscent of Banbury, York North could be thought of as the opposite end of th[ ]GC connection, with a preponderance of ex-Great Central regulars often on shed in the early 'sixties – 'V2s', 'B1s[ ]'9Fs' and 'WDs'. At least another five engine class types are discernible on closer examination. The shed's open-ai[ ]nature, with perhaps a raw nor'-easter, would make these enginemen's task a thankless one, albeit workin[ ]alongside hot boilers!

Twenty-six years later, on 3 June 1989, the NRM cosmetics as applied externally to the roundhouse are evident[ ]In the open display area, replica ex-GWR engine *Iron Duke* receives a work-out, and standing on the much altere[ ]BR layout are two Class '08' 'pilots' up against the buffers of the fuelling point. An engineers' inspection uni[ ]completes the scene. *Both ART*

YORK NORTH SHED YARD (2): Class 'A1' Peppercorn 'Pacific' No 60138 *Boswell* remained a 50A, York, engine from nationalisation until its demise in October 1965. Here, in January 1963, and still a picture of good health in the early winter sunset, she stands in the North Yard being turned for a northbound duty. Behind stands Class '40' English Electric No D390 and a sister, the eventual successors to many of the duties of the 'A1s'.

On 7 April 1991 the former turntable site is now a ReadyMix Concrete depot. The point of reference is the shed to the left of *Boswell*'s tender, together with the distant tall tower. Alan Thompson couldn't repeat the exact location today and it will be noticed that he was several feet to the left. In the background can be seen a 'Pacer' DMU *en route* from Harrogate along a now much simplified section of ECML. *Both ART*

YORK NORTH SHED INTERIOR (1): Here we see two of York North's most celebrated responsibilities. The 'P3', or 'J27', Class engine on the left needs no introduction . . . No 65894 rarely strayed from 50A from the mid-'fifties through to the mid-'sixties, when it joined its many sisters on Tyneside to momentarily become a genuine mineral leading engine (instead of a branch line pick-up engine) among the pitheaps of County Durham. In September 1967 she was selected by founder members of the North Eastern Locomotive Preservation Group as the remaining engine in the best condition to be towed away to Tyne Dock shed for preservation. The engine to the right on No 13 road is Class 'V2' No 60847 *St Peter's School York AD627*. The pair were hardly ever seen in a grubby condition and 60847 had just been cleaned when Alan Thompson came by in 1963. The wall behind the engines was once the area of Nos 1 and 2 sheds, demolished in 1957-58 at the same time that the shed shown was remodelled as a straight shed and re-roofed.

Behind the wall today stands the NRM maintenance area where semi-renovated engines can sometimes be glimpsed. On display roads 12 and 13 in the much cleaner interior of the NRM in October 1989 are the Stirling 'Single' once again, re-sited from the old museum, and ex-GWR 2-8-0 heavy freight engine No 2818. *Both ART*

The nameplate portrait above was captured on the same visit. We have to thank the famous school of the same name for permission to go in to record the 'present' situation of the nameplate (left) which is in fact that from the left-hand side of the engine. *Both ART*

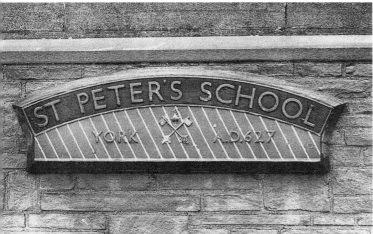

Finally, the up-to-date scene in this part of the NRM shows the new roof structure finalised, with the side wall ready to once again accommodate the museum's fine collection of engine nameplates. April 1991. *KG*

YORK NORTH SHED INTERIOR (2): A corner of the 1957 remodelled No 4 shed on a sleepy Sunday afternoon in March 1963 sees the resident engines, Class 'K1' No 62009 and Class 'B1' No 61062, quietly raising steam in readiness for early morning Monday turns of duty on roads No 1 and 2 respectively. The absence of smoke cowls and few gaps in the glass panelling soon resulted in 'soup-like' conditions!

The same spot after 32 years, but now with the roof area clean and painted, highlighting the old steam era lines in 'glorious technicolour'. The previously windowed area has been boarded up and the concrete trusses are now wrapped for safety. The *Rocket* replica perhaps takes pride of place, and behind is the statue of 'Geordie' Stephenson, looking seriously down upon the visitors. Furness Railway *Coppernob* has now replaced the 'B1' on No 2 road and the Grand Junction Railway's 2-2-2 makes up the trio with the Weatherhill engine forming a backcloth. *Both ART*

YORK NORTH SHED INTERIOR (3): A trio of Gresley mixed traffic class 'V2' engines line up in May 1963 on 21, 22 and 23 roads; No 60968 was one of those to go in the summer 1963 clear-out, while 60855 was withdrawn the following April and 60833 a month later. 50A's allocation of this type totalled 30 in 1950, had dropped by only two 10 years later but by 1965 was down to 1 in the run-up to the extinction of steam diagrams on the ECML.

This central turntable displayed a motley collection of exhibits when viewed on 3 June 1989. Occupying the same roads were LNER electric No 26020 *Tommy*, a Class 'O4' shunting engine, and a modern push-pull-fitted Mark III coach, with green/yellow-coated 'Deltic' 55002 and the rear of 'A4' 'Pacific' No 60022 (now back to No 4468) *Mallard*. *Both RT*

Following the 1989-91 reconstruction work, the NRM stands ready again for the return of the nation's most famous railway engines, the 70-foot Mundt turntable retained as the focal point for engine displays. We were privileged to be allowed in to record the NRM in this condition — it will probably never be seen like this again! *KG*

YORK NORTH SHED INTERIOR (4): Perhaps epitomising the description 'Cathedrals of Steam', such a view will surely bring a lump to the throat of those who can momentarily recall the smell and feel of such an emotive atmosphere. Early 1991 news that the fine surviving steam age roundhouse at Barrow Hill has had its future assured raises the question as to whether this evocative atmosphere will again be engineered one day – for photo sessions, or just for the pure visual/sensory effects. Preparing for 'backshift' duties shortly before Christmas 1962, Class 'V2' No 60961 keeps company with self-cleaning Class 'A2/3' No 60524 *Herringbone*. The latter, soon to be transferred away to St Margarets (Edinburgh) then shortly afterwards to Aberdeen (Ferryhill) and never to return to an English depot, ended her days as a Polmadie engine in February 1965.

Wind the clock on a further 27 years and we now find that the pride of the nation, world steam record holder *Mallard* (unfortunately tender facing) has replaced No 60828 on road 19, flanked by type successor 'Deltic' No 55002, while *Tommy* has replaced *Herringbone* in slot No 21. Also seen to *Mallard's* left is the rear of Midland Compound No 1000. The wrapped concrete struts are perhaps an indication of the dangerous state of the 1957 roof, now replaced. *Both ART*

YORK YARDS: An area not seen by the ECML traveller, York freight avoiding lines once traversed an area with the hallmarks of heavy industry and in complete contrast to the refined station surroundings. From north to south first to be passed was the sugar factory, then Skelton sidings, the Carriage Works and its own yard until ultimately you arrived at this point, with the wagon works on the right linked by an elliptical footbridge to the south end of the Carriage Works area near Cleveland Place. Beyond the footbridge is the broad expanse of the NER goods and mineral sidings, collectively becoming known as the York Yards. On 8 September 1971 Class '25' No 7561 is seen leaving the yard with a mixed rake of North Eastern coke for Toton Yard. *John H. Cooper Smith*

Today the footbridge has gone and York Yard South signal box has been eclipsed by the modern SSI York Signalling Centre, itself now controlling 200 route miles and linked up on Monday 13 May 1991 with the next signal box to the north, at Newcastle! *KG*

YORK STATION (I): We now move to the main station, and we could not let the opportunity pass to show some detail from the station's focal point, the east end of the overbridge and the Station Master's 'glass palace' (the station signal box until 1951), seen here on 5 October 1965. There is an immense amount of rich detail at this point that under normal circumstances might be quickly bypassed by travellers. Few look up to see how the cast iron NER coat-of-arms is incorporated within each roof spandrel, or even notice the way in which the clock is held by a carefully designed lattice bracket. On a less serious note is the notice between the two seated men: 'Please help keep the station tidy by not feeding the pigeons'. *BR*

Happily the station at this point has altered little and a 'present' view was thus thought unnecessary. Motive power, however, is a different story . . .

YORK STATION (2): Four eras of northbound ECML motive power seen under the Victorian majesty of York's 1877 train shed. On 7 September 1963, Class 'V2' No 60885 of Darlington MPD awaits the 'board' with the 19.28 Sunday evening Leeds–Darlington train. *ART*

Eight years on, almost to the day, on 8 September 1971, and the 22-strong 'Deltic' fleet is in full control of the ECML top-link passenger diagrams. Prior to TOPS renumbering, No 9013 *The Black Watch* has just opened up with her twin Napier engines to make the noise for so long synonymous with ECML expresses. She is working the 08.00 King's Cross–Edinburgh and has been given the 'M' display in the theatre-style indicator at platform 5 for the main line northwards. *John H. Cooper Smith*

Our third view at this well-photographed location is of the 'Deltic' successor, Class '43' Intercity 125 No 43082 leading the 10.00 King's Cross–Edinburgh train on 3 June 1989. By now the necessity to make all railway infrastructure accountable has resulted in many station through roads, such as these at York, being removed because of their inability to get suitable sector maintenance sponsorship. *ART*

Right up to date, and only just in time for this publication, is this picture of only the second down Anglo-Scottish express in the care of the new-look Class '91' electrics, on Wednesday 12 June 1991. The new service was due to begin on Monday 10 June, but overhead power supply problems in the Benton to Morpeth area, near Newcastle, prevented through running to Scotland until the day after, when the 11.00 service from King's Cross was the first through Anglo-Scottish train by ECML electric. This is the same service on its second day of running (see page 4 for a view of the first historic run north of York), and will be the look at York for some time to come! *KG*

YORK'S TWO STATIONS: This *circa* 1910 view encompasses both of York's stations. On the left of the Bar Walls is the 1877 station of the present day with the many-chimneyed Royal Station Hotel beyond. To the right, inside the Walls, is the original Queen Street station, with a small 0-6-0 pilot engine shuffling four- and six-wheel clerestory vans and coaches. Opened in 1841 and funded by the York & North Midland and the Great North of England companies, Queen Street succeeded a temporary 1839 terminus which was on a site close to the later 1877 station. Built at a time when it was thought a terminus would do, George Hudson's ambitions meant that a new through station was soon urgently needed, this time more sensibly sited *outside* the City Walls. In the right background is the grand NER Headquarters building of 1906. It's 10.25 am by the station clock and there's hardly a soul about — perhaps it's a Sunday morning! *BR*

In 1991 the view outside the Walls has changed but little, while Queen Street station has been replaced by BR's new Hudson House (see subsequent pages). *KG*

YORK QUEEN STREET STATION (1) in 1951 when, as part of the Festival of Britain celebrations, the brand new class-leader *Britannia* headed a line-up of the latest and (then) best locomotives. It can be seen that the old station of 1841 was still in use, and in fact remained so until 1966 when the track was lifted to make way for the Civil Engineering and Infrastructure HQ to be called Hudson House. The track occupied by No 70000 was used as a Motorail loading bay until this facility was eventually moved to platform 1 in the present station. *JWA*

In the summer of 1991 the driveway that replaced the Motorail bay skirts Hudson House now dominating the skyline where once stood the pride of the York & North Midland Railway. *KG*

YORK QUEEN STREET STATION (2): A broad view in about 1925 over the old station on what appears as a wet foggy day. It is thought that the old hotel, at the end of the train shed, would by now have been in use as office premises with the two parallel buildings, on either side of the station, used by station staff for letters, parcels and storage. The frail cast-iron pillars look inadequate for the heavy hotch-potch of roofing. It can be seen that the roof adjoining the City Wall embankment has been removed since 1910 (see page 96) — it may be that it was proving too much temptation to those with roof-climbing aspirations! *BR*

The panorama from the Bar Walls today shows how the Clean Air Acts have certainly changed York's atmosphere, allowing us to see more clearly the former NER (now BR) Headquarters building and what remains of Queen Street station in the foreground. The railway hotel of 1853 now forms a major part of the York Headquarters overspill, and is known as the 'West Offices'. *KG*

The remaining Queen Street station awning is a listed structure and is seen, together with the station platform remains, in April 1991, viewed from the surrounding offices. *KG*

Turning through 180 degrees from the views of Queen Street station opposite, we see roadways where rails once drove a passage through the Walls and over the site of the temporary 1839 station. On the left is the former Queen Street Works, adjacent to the home of the old York Railway Museum, and on the right the south end of the present-day station. *KG*

YORK, TANNER'S MOAT: It would need a separate book to describe adequately the wealth of historical detail glimpsed from this City Wall viewpoint. The photograph's raison d'être is only just visible on the far right-hand side — the old Tanner's Moat factory of Seebohm Rowntree, prior to his move out to Haxby Road ready for further expansion towards today's international super-company. It just so happens that the commissioned photographer inadvertently recorded one of the most unforgettable and important railway scenes to date, and of a quality that would quite depress the electronic lightweight contemporary photographer!

At this time, *circa* 1868, the original but temporary terminus of the Y&NMR (opened on 29 May 1839 just outside the City Walls) had given way to the more permanent 1841 Queen Street station, but an immediate shortage of local carriage sidings saw the company push past alongside the 1841 building to Tanner's Moat and Lendal Bridge, the result of which is seen here. The three sidings form a strange and cramped counterpoint to the wall and roadway and, although it is not recorded, must have been a dangerous and irritating addition for pedestrians passing through. From today's viewpoint it is an appalling aesthetic shock to see so many 'bumbler boxes' made up of stove pipes, wrought iron and open luggage racks lined up within shouting distance of one of the world's greatest religious and architectural institutions — the Minster of York. We can only surmise what might have happened had the Minster itself lay in the way of George Hudson! Beyond the sleeper stockade behind the buffer-stop is the then small wall opening for pedestrians and horses, later expanded to become today's Leeman Road thoroughfare leading into Rougier Street and thence George Hudson Street. Across the River Ouse is Museum Street, leading the eye up to the Minster. The nearest coach destination board reads 'YORK–NORMANTON' and, curiously, there isn't one person out strolling.

We leave readers to 'spot the differences'! *BR/KG*

101

YORK STATION SOUTH (I): This view of York station south in about 1920 compares quite badly with today's cleaner lines, especially considering that BR have been criticised from time to time by Council planners because of 'heavy' electrification structures! The illustration is a nightmare by today's health and safety requirements and the raised wooden board walks would certainly not have passed muster as authorised walking routes due to their proximity to running lines.

The view nevertheless is at a fascinating point where much history has been made. For example, to the far right stands the Queen Street loco shed, formerly the Works Boiler Shop of the York & North Midland Railway. This shed area was taken over by the L&YR and survived into LMS ownership until deserted by that company in 1932 in favour of the South shed roundhouse seen to the extreme left. The old Queen Street shed was regardless still used as a makeshift stabling point for various departmental rolling-stock, that is until 1968 when the roof finally capitulated on top of a rather venerable example of an Officer's Saloon. Its life span was from 1909 to 1951, finally becoming obsolete with the then revolutionary update in signalling practices called 'electro-pneumatic' operation. The second point with accommodation for 295 levers and a host of box lads busily recording times in the train register. Its life span was from 1909 to 1951, finally becoming obsolete with the then revolutionary update in signalling practices called 'electro-pneumatic' operation. The second span was from 1909 to 1951, finally becoming obsolete with the then revolutionary update in signalling practices called 'electro-pneumatic' operation. The second gantry attached to the far end of the signal box was also a busy staff footbridge, leading across to Branches Yard and Coal Depots, Leeman Road Goods Depots and the Midland locomotive depot. *BR*

The 1877 NER station is surrounded by steam activity, whilst in today's view the graceful and now listed train shed shows up clearly from an equivalent but safer position! The simplified track layout has resulted from two major resignalling schemes, 1951 and more recently in 1989 when the 1951 replacement of the old signal box illustrated itself gave way to the latest signalling technology, solid state interlocking and computer-controlled auto route setting coupled to main timetable data. Today's view was taken on 5 April 1991 and it can be seen that Queen Street loco shed is now the southern extent of the 'park and ride' facility associated with the station. *KG*

YORK STATION SOUTH (2): The eight occupants of the Locomotive Yard signal box pause briefly below its six gas lamps whilst the photographer catches a scene of typical 1940s working conditions. As might be expected, stout shoes and thick socks were essential in such establishments to combat the wintry draughts emanating from the gaps in both the boardwalk and the lever spaces. *BR*

This illustration, intended more to show the 'past' layout in action, is also interesting in that it affords a view of the 1932-abandoned LMS locomotive shed at Queen Street on the right. The two 'scissors' crossings are clearly seen between platforms 10 and 11 (left), and alongside platform 9 (right). At the far left is the island platform 15/16 (now 10/11) and visible above it are the windows of the just completed 1951 power box, the latest technology of the day.

It is 22 February 1951, at a time when the up 'Northumbrian' was in the Heaton links and 52B Class 'A1' 'Pacific' No 60126 *Sir Vincent Raven* weaves out of platform 8 to take the up fast line for King's Cross. *BR*

YORK STATION SOUTH (3): A further perspective on the south end of the station, this time from the Holgate 'train-watching' platform. It is June 1958 and 'Jubilee' No 45579 *Punjab* leaves with a Newcastle–Birmingham express, with a Leeds-bound DMU a short head behind. Incidentally, this DMU was one of the few seen in the North East with a roof-mounted train description indicator display panel.

On 5 April 1991 a Class '156' 'Sprinter' leaves for Manchester over the much simplified trackwork of today's railway. *Both ART*

HOLGATE BRIDGE: Bank Hall (Liverpool) 'Jubilee' Class No 45698 *Mars* picks up its feet momentarily after restarting a Liverpool train of all-maroon stock on a fine summer June day in 1959.

The same services on 6 April 1991 are in the hands of anonymous Class '158' DMUs wearing the first two-tone blue livery of Regional Railways 'Express' trains. Holgate Bridge has since been raised 1 foot (300mm to be exact) to provide the clearance needed for overhead line equipment, and the once well-manicured approach to Holgate Excursion platform in the background is a weed-edged access track — only a small portion of support wall remains. As for Holgate Dock to the left, with a bit of imagination this could well become a 'nice little earner' for BR. The regular gaggle of 'spotters' here bring deckchairs and portable TVs, whilst tripod-mounted video cameras jostle for space! *Both ART*

HOLGATE EXCURSION PLATFORM (1): We couldn't leave York without a view of the NER locomen's favourite, the NER 'R' Class. Their appearance in 1900 had a profound impact on the NER timetable and as quickly as 1902 (until about 1914) the class earned the reputation of 'flyers' as the engines scheduled to haul the 12.20 pm Newcastle–Bristol express. 'The fastest train in the British Empire' was a title earned for running over the Darlington–York section at 61 mph. The 60-strong class roamed far and wide over the ex-NER area, even making regular rambles over the Border Counties line into Scotland. After the Second World War they congregated upon Selby MPD to work semi-fast services and summer trains on the Bridlington, Filey and Scarborough routes, and were ultimately responsible for haulage of workers' trains from Doncaster and Selby to York and Rowntree's Halt. Whilst the Rowntree's workers' train shown here approaches York in 1956, the painters are busy on the overbridge. *Bob Payne*

Wind the clock on 35 years and 6 April 1991 reveals 'Sprinter' Unit 156475 entering York with a service from Halifax. The footbridge has been replaced and Holgate platform edge is no more, but the adjacent residents now have a fine unrestricted view over this busy piece of railway (not that many will appreciate the change!). *ART*

HOLGATE EXCURSION PLATFORM (2): Seen from the opposite side of the line, and a little nearer York station, is Thompson rebuilt 'B16' Class 4-6-0 No 61464, recently ex-Works from Darlington, speeding into York with an express from Leeds composed of some very mixed stock in about 1959.

Also heading for York with a service from Leeds on 5 April 1991 is red and cream 'Metro-Train' Unit No 155344, while overhead the most dramatic addition to the scene is the ECML 'knitting'. *Both ART*

DRINGHOUSES YARD, south of York, had been ripe for modernisation when improvements to bring it into line with semi-automatic hump shunting of block sections were authorised at the end of the 'fifties. By 1961 the remodelled yard opened, but the dramatic turnaround of rail freight from its common user status to the convenience-only block-load traffic of the 'eighties sounded its death knell. The yard clung on almost entirely due to Rowntree-Mackintosh's contribution, but with their switch to juggernaut lorries in April 1987 the closure of Dringhouses Yard soon followed. Here we see it two years after modernisation as a block load of early fuel tanks from Teesside pulls away on the up slow line behind 'V2' No 60961 sporting a fully-fitted freight headlight code.

Today the houses remain, but occupied by fewer railway families than before! The hump yard is levelled but is still used by the Civil Engineer to stockpile up to 3,000 tons of spoilt ballast (a remnant of the 1989 York remodelling scheme). Only one lighting tower remains to say what has gone before. On 5 April 1991 a similar flow of tanks to Immingham goes south over what was once the down main line and which is now a bi-directional route. *Both ART*

110

WHELDRAKE, DVLR : Finally in this York section we turn to the Derwent Valley Light Railway, opened in 1913 and branching off the York–Scarborough line at Burton Lane Junction, meandering east to Murton Lane, then turning south towards Cliffe Common to join up with the Bridlington–Selby route. Class 'J21' 0-6-0 No 65078 has arrived with an RCTS special at Wheldrake in the early 'fifties, possibly the most used station and approximately midway along the 16-mile route. The line somehow escaped nationalisation and scraped a living with rural traffic until a make-or-break stage was reached in 1976. The next year a steam service was installed to revive fortunes and the then recently renovated Class 'J72' shunting loco No 69023 was acquired by the railway operators. After some initial success the line closed on 27 September 1981 but is currently the subject of yet another rail revival scheme. *JWA*

On 4 June 1989 the building is surprisingly intact and seemingly belongs to a Government Department. Gone is the raised boardwalk platform, the land having been levelled before returning to nature. *ART*

South to Selby

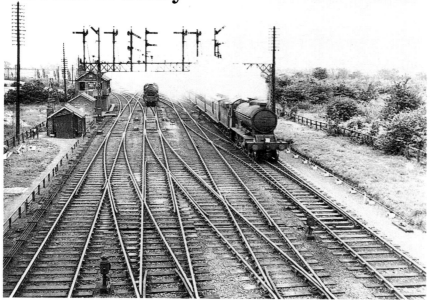

CHALONERS WHIN: Because of the scissors crossover between platforms 8 and 9 at York (see page 105) and the four-track exit to the south to Chaloners Whin junction, 2 miles south of York station, ECML and Sheffield/Leeds direction trains could be dispatched independently and many a pair has raced to this once diverging point. With the opening of the Selby Diversion in 1983 the junction ceased to be, and the location where ECML trains diverge is now at Colton (see page 114). However, this does not in any way curtail neck-and-neck running over this stretch as all the routes are now bi-directional. Our 1949 illustration shows a Class 'B16' engine two coaches ahead of a Midland line 'Black Five' on the approach to York from the Leeds and Sheffield directions respectively. *JWA*

Today's view, taken from the nearest vantage point (since the bridge parapet is now 7 feet high) tells the story of the re-aligned and simplified former junction. The old route to the left towards Bishopthorpe (see the cover picture) has returned to nature, the signal box and peripheral cabins are totally razed, the overall gantry long gone . . . only the far fencing is a tangible link with the days when the LNER raced the LMS in and out of York. *ART*

A superb ground-level view of the gantry and beyond it the bridge from which the 1949 view opposite was taken; in July 1948 LNER 'B16' 4-6-0 No 1441 heads south with an up express goods. Note that, from the left, the second, third, fifth, sixth and eighth 'dolls' on the gantry are still NER slotted posts. *E. R. Wethersett/BR*

COLTON JUNCTION: Until recently not a recognised location on the East Coast Main Line, Colton was chosen as the point where the new Selby Diversion would leave the former Sheffield and Leeds route to bypass Selby and rejoin the original ECML at Templehirst. We were lucky enough to find an early stake-out view taken during the 1977 route planning process, which is reproduced here. *BR*

Stepping back a little, it can be seen that a new bridge has joined the original by 5 April 1991, beneath which a 'Pacer' on a Selby service is about to pass on the new ECML alignment. It will diverge again at Hambleton Junction North to travel down the Leeds–Selby route. The railway cottages remain, overlooking a wide expanse of high-speed routes. *ART*

Above A view of Colton Junction showing the smooth high-speed alignment of the divergence. *BR*

Right An aerial view of Templehirst Junction at the south end of the Selby Diversion, under construction in the winter of 1980/81. An up HST travels along the original line from Selby, heading for the bridge over the River Aire. *BR*

115

SELBY DIVERSION: The 1977 stake-out for the proposed ECML diversion took the new railway across this rural road, over the Bishops Dike and through a part of the Bishops Wood between Cawood and Sherburn in Elmet. *BR*

The present-day photograph taken on 6 April 1991 shows the resulting re-arrangement of the topography. The road has been truncated and realigned (behind the field of vision). The Bishops Dike can be seen on its new course swinging to the left with a new bankside still apparently a patch of flattened raw clay. The Bishops Wood, barely visible above the new railway, now has a swathe of shining permanent way cut through its north-west corner, seen here being traversed by the Healey Mills–Gartcosh coal container train led by Class '37' No 37108, since moved into the DCAA-Civil Engineers Anglia pool of locos. *ART*

CHURCH FENTON STATION on the York & North Midland route between Milford and York opened in 1847 to coincide with the opening of the branch north-westwards to Harrogate. It served a community of little more than 1,000 people at the turn of the century, but passengers figures remained stable enough to persuade the authorities at York to authorise expenditure of over £7,000 for a new station including intricate station awnings seen here in the early 'fifties. Class 'J27' No 65875, then of Selby, is seen taking coke empties southbound towards the LMR hand-over yards in the Milford area. *JWA*

It is perhaps surprising to find that the awning over island platform 2 and 3 in our March 1990 illustration looks in better condition with new glass added, but it is an illusion because the sad fact is that the roofing was in the process of removal, the contractors having already begun dismantling the main roof sections. Metals sector No 37232, obviously on loan to the Civil Engineer's Department for the weekend, hauls ballast empties in the direction of Normanton. *Roger Hill*

CHURCH FENTON SOUTH JUNCTION: As well as the line to Harrogate, Church Fenton was also the junction for a wide south-westerly chord linking with the Leeds and Selby route. Our South Junction view of 1954 shows the South Yorkshire line stretching to the south around a graceful wide curve, whilst York-based Class 'WD' 2-8-0 No 90424 returns a permanent way tracklaying train towards York from the Leeds direction, during an unhurried Sunday afternoon. *JWA*

Apart from the high-speed crossovers on the simplified South Yorkshire route, signalling modernisation in line with IECC/SSI, and the not unexpected disappearance of the South Junction signal box, little has changed in over 36 years. On 13 January 1990 Roger Hill found the bankside bushes precluded an exact re-enactment whilst photographing a Class '155' DMU *en route* from Manchester to York. The railway cottages behind still make to this day an excellent viewing gallery across the wide junction! *Roger Hill*

GASCOIGNE WOOD: The first route into York, steered by George Hudson, arrived from Milford Junction in 1839. It was here that the York & North Midland crossed the Leeds & Selby Railway of 1834, and this paved the way for the location to be transformed from a once quiet hamlet on the edge of a wood to an important inter-area freight transfer point on the Selby route, eventually forming a junction round to Milford and the point where North Midland traffic was taken on to the Humber and East Yorkshire at Gascoigne Wood. Here we see train 193 taking the east to south curve with an East Yorkshire–Midlands excursion on August Bank Holiday 1954. *JWA*

If not for the retained signal box the current view could have been taken somewhere else. The eastern neck of the mineral yard now accommodates part of the spreading Selby coalfield. Passing the old signal box on 10 March 1990 is a Hull–Leeds Class '156' 'Super Sprinter' looking a lot like a model train-set on this glorious sunny evening. In the foreground is the curve round to Milford Junction. No sign remains of the railway community. *Roger Hill*

MILFORD JUNCTION was at the lower apex of the triangle, and was the point where inter-regional passenger trains bound for East Coast resorts would often change locomotives. Looking south up the main line, here is a case in question as the deposed LM Region 'Crab' No 42847, of Derby MPD, stands in the siding whilst Scarborough Class 'B16' No 61445 drops back on to its Manchester–Scarborough train (No 190) in July 1958. *JWA*

Asking Roger Hill to repeat the photograph was in itself easy; little did he anticipate the detective work needed to help relocate the same spot. Eventually Roger inquired of a retired railwayman who led him to this place and showed him where the base of the water column still stood. If he should read this — thank you! This February 1990 photograph clearly illustrates the anonymity of the spot as MGR empties are hurried back to the Durham coalfields. *Roger Hill*

MONK FRYSTON, south of Milford Junction, owed its existence to the routing of the York and Normanton section of the York & North Midland through here in 1840. It was another 64 years (1902) before the station was constructed at a cost of £639, and the less convenient station at Milford Junction was closed in consequence. The 'past' picture, taken in about 1950, shows the extensive sidings stretching towards South Milford. A loading gauge together with a loading dock is just visible to the right, the location where once grain and bulk vegetables were loaded in season. The LMS connection is very evident here as Beyer Garratt 2-6-6-2 No 47982 takes the Midland route with a substantial train of coal empties for replenishment in the South Yorkshire coalfield. *JWA*

Today's scene confirms that rail interest in power station supplies has supported retention of the mineral holding sidings near Milford and some associated expensive crossover junctions, at a time when they are becoming rarer. The goods loading dock remains, together with a half-hidden Goods Agent's house, whilst 47809 *Finsbury Park* threads the layout with a York–South Coast Intercity 'Saga' special conveying a rebogied BG (NEA) at each end for luggage. Monk Fryston lost its passenger service in September 1959 and goods facilities officially ended on 4 May 1964. *Roger Hill*

HAMBLETON has seen a return to railway prominence since becoming the crossing point of the re-aligned ECML under and on to the Leeds–Selby–Hull route. The station arrived early on the railway map, in 1834, and closure came for this rural byway on 14 September 1959. Four years before, John Armstrong recorded Selby-based Class 'G5' No 67250 drifting westbound into the rustic platform, whilst the downside platform is quickly swept past by an 'A4' 'Pacific' hauling a diverted ECML train. *JWA*

The express in fact pre-empts the ultimate route of the main line, and the present view of Hambleton taken on 10 March 1990 shows that the station site is now on a west to south chord connecting the 1834 Selby route to the re-routed ECML. 'Super Sprinter' No 156475 is seen on the Selby route with a Manchester–Hull service about to cross the ECML (indicated by the distant overhead wires). *Roger Hill*

SELBY SWING BRIDGE: The first railway to reach Selby was the line from Leeds in 1834, and although planned to continue through to Hull, the small matter of bridging the River Ouse presented quite a few early technical problems, enough certainly to delay further progress for six years. With the continuation to Hull came a second Selby station west of the first and in alignment with the first railway bridge of bascule construction, ie raised and lowered by counterpoise, seen here *circa* 1880 with the railway pointing skywards on the elevated section.

The age of much larger iron ships and great advancements on Tyneside in the art of hydraulic engineering were the major factors that hastened the end of the first Selby bridge. The construction of the 1891 swinging bridge also gave the opportunity to rebuild the second station to incorporate the vital loop lines off the fast; a further final enlargement followed in 1899-1900. *Both BR*

SELBY STATION (1): Curiously this once main-line route was not the original choice but a consequence of the NER applying to the Government, in 1863, for powers to construct a new direct line from Chaloners Whin to Barlby, just north of Selby, to join the Selby–Hull route. This was in order to bypass the need to share metals with the less than sympathetic Lancashire & Yorkshire company between Knottingly and Askern Junction. The new line via Selby opened in January 1871 and lasted just over 100 years before the BR/NCB Selby Diversion brought a reversion to a route closely resembling the 1839 profile. Selby is therefore where it began – off the main East Coast route — but it is compensated by its local shuttle service to and from York. In ECML days, crossing the Ouse at the north end of Selby station is Class 'J11' No 64397 of Colwick. The clutter of railway 'furniture' here is quite remarkable, and surely a modeller's delight! *JWA*

The not inconsiderable 'throat' problem of the swing bridge, the quite severe speed restriction and the little problem of wiring a moveable bridge for electrification were all exacerbated by the fact that the Masters of passing shipping frequently found this the place to have steerage problems! Thus BR had no hesitation in accepting the NCB's kind financial assistance for the re-routing of the ECML away from Selby! Seen in January 1990, a first-generation DMU enters Selby with a Hull–York service; perhaps a far cry from the roar of an ECML express, but Selby retains a station of great character and an important point on a route regenerated by North Transpennine 'Super Sprinters'. *Roger Hill*

SELBY STATION (2): Our 'past' picture, from 1952, shows Class 'V2' No 60853, of New England MPD, taking the through line with a down semi-fast express for York (note the lower quadrant signal repeaters). The station had grown over the years via various re-alignments reflecting the metamorphosis of the swing bridge just beyond the north end. The final form, reached by 1900, may perhaps account for the double reverse curve, well illustrated here. The platforms themselves provided slow loop lines, but the swing bridge was an every-present delaying factor because, regardless of mining subsidence, river traffic had priority over rail movements. *JWA*

Today's view, taken on 13 January 1990, shows a most excellent restored period piece in the same mould perhaps as Hexham or even Stirling! As a Manchester–Hull Class '156' visits, it occurs to the onlooker that although Selby people complain of missing out on East Coast expresses, their absence has prolonged the charm of their extremely uncluttered local station with its minimum of infrastructure requirements. *Roger Hill*

SELBY STATION (3): This view of the south end of Selby station in 1954 perhaps conjures up for many of us memories of holidays to the Yorkshire coast whereby the local brought us to the main-line connection. Resting in the bay platform, Class 'G5' No 67286 stands with a recently arrived push-pull service from Goole; its fireman nonchalantly observes passengers transferring to a Hull–Leeds train with Class 'D49' No 62701 *Derbyshire* at its head, and based at Hull Botanic Gardens MPD. *JWA*

On 13 January 1990 a Regional Railways Class '141' 'Pacer' DMU is employed on the same duties as No 67286, while a Class '156', part of the North Transpennine 'arm' of Regional Railways, has replaced the 'D49' on the cross-country route. The swan-neck gas lamps and the large concrete flower-pot focal points have been replaced by cleaner lines which have in no way detracted from the station's character. It seems, however, that today's passengers are less encouraged to sit out in the elements! *Roger Hill*

INDEX OF LOCATIONS